NATIONAL 4 & 5

HISTORY

HITLER AND NAZI GERMANY 1919–1939

SECOND EDITION

John A. Kerr

The Publishers would like to thank the following for permission to reproduce copyright material:

Photo credits: p.3 (left) © Popperfoto/Getty Images, (right) © Popperfoto/Getty Images; **p.4** © Kaethe Kollwitz, courtesy of BPK-Bildagentur; **p.5** © UNT Libraries Government Documents Department; **p.10** © Granger, NYC/TopFoto; **p.11** (left) © Bain News Service/Buyenlarge/Getty Images, (right) © World History Archive/TopFoto; **p.13** © Pictorial Press Ltd/Alamy Stock Photo; **p.14** (left) © George Rinhart/Corbis via Getty Images, (right) © National Geographic Stock: Vintage Collection/GRANGER — All rights reserved. **p.21** © akg-images/Alamy Stock Photo; **p.22** © Chronicle/Alamy Stock Photo; **p.23** © Chronicle/Alamy Stock Photo; **p.27** © Deutsches Historisches Museum, Berlin/A. Psille; **p.28** © Universal History Archive/Getty Images; **p.29** © steheap/Fotolia; **p.33** © Keystone/Getty Images; **p.34** (top) © Keystone/Getty Images, (bottom) © Private Collection/Peter Newark Pictures/Bridgeman Images; **p.39** (top left) © Keystone/Getty Images, (top right) © Keystone/Getty Images, (bottom) © Hulton Archive/Getty Images; **p.41** © Nick Koudis/Getty Images; **p.44** © Keystone/Getty Images; **p.46** © Photo12/UIG/Getty Images; **p.50** © Chronicle/Alamy Stock Photo; **p.51** © INTERFOTO/Alamy Stock Photo; **p.52** © akg-images; **p.53** © Punch Limited/TopFoto.co.uk; **p.57** © Fox Photos/Getty Images; **p.58** © Express Syndication/British Cartoon Archive; **p.59** © Mondadori Portfolio/Getty Images; **p.63** (top) © Banco de México Diego Rivera Frida Kahlo Museums Trust, Mexico, D.F./DACS 2018/Topfoto, (bottom) © Eye Ubiquitous/UIG via Getty Images; **p.64** (top) © Popperfoto/Getty Images, (bottom) © Chronicle/Alamy Stock Photo; **p.65** (left) © PA Photos/TopFoto, (right) © Guy Corbishley/Alamy Stock Photo; **p.69** (top) © triocean/Fotolia, (bottom) © George (Jürgen) Wittenstein/akg; **p.70** © BPK; **p.73** © Zec/Mirrorpix; **p.75** © Granger, NYC; **p.80** (left) © Chronicle/Alamy Stock Photo, (right) © Anthony Potter Collection/Getty Images; **p.81** (top) © Hulton Archive/Getty Images, (bottom) © Mary Evans Picture Library/Alamy; **p.82** © Voller Ernst/ullstein bild via Getty Images; **p.86** © Albert Harlingue/Roger Viollet/Getty Images; **p.87** (top left) © Galerie Bilderwelt/Getty Images, (top right) © C. and M. History Pictures/Alamy Stock Photo, (bottom) © Popperfoto/Getty Images; **p.88** © Everett Collection Historical/Alamy Stock Photo; **p.91** © Mary Evans/Sueddeutsche Zeitung Photo; **p.92** © Mondadori via Getty Images; **p.93** © Universal History Archive/Getty Images; **p.94** © Everett Collection Historical/Alamy Stock Photo; **p.98** © CBW/Alamy Stock Photo; **p.99** (left and right) © INTERFOTO/Alamy Stock Photo; **p.100** © BPK.

Acknowledgements: **pp.5 & 7** extracts from *Out of the Night: The Memoir of Richard Julius Herman Krebs Alias Jan Valtin* by Jan Valtin (AK Press, 1994). Reproduced by permission of AK Press; **p.22** extract from *The Autobiography of a German Rebel* by Toni Sender (Routledge, 1940); **p.51** extract from *The Course of German History* by A.J.P. Taylor (Hamish Hamilton, 1945); **p.90** extract from *Women at War, 1914–18* by Arthur Marwick (Fontana, 1977); **p.90** extract from *I Knew Hitler: The Lost Testimony by a Survivor from the Night of the Long Knives* by Kurt G.W. Ludecke and edited by Bob Carruthers. Reproduced by permission of Pen & Sword Books; **p.93** extract from *My Years in Germany* by Martha Dodd (Gollancz, 1939); **p.94** extract from *The Nazi Seizure of Power: The Experience of a Single German Town 1922–1945* by William Sheridan Allen (Echo Point Books & Media, 2014). Copyright © 1965, 1984, 2014 William Sheridan Allen; **p.94** Excerpt from *"The Good War": An Oral History of World War II* – Copyright © 1984 by Studs Terkel. Reprinted by permission of The New Press. www.thenewpress.com; **p.96** extract from *The Naked Years: Growing Up in Nazi Germany* by Marianne MacKinnon (Corgi, 1989).

Orders: please contact Hachette UK Distribution, Hely Hutchinson Centre, Milton Road, Didcot, Oxfordshire, OX11 7HH. Telephone: +44 (0)1235 827827. Email education@hachette.co.uk. Lines are open from 9 a.m. to 5 p.m., Monday to Friday. You can also order through our website: www.hoddereducation.co.uk. If you have queries or questions that aren't about an order, you can contact us at hoddergibson@hodder.co.uk

First published in 2013 © John A. Kerr

This second edition published in 2018 by
Hodder Gibson, an imprint of Hodder Education,
An Hachette UK Company
211 St Vincent Street
Glasgow G2 5QY

Impression number 5 4
Year 2022 2021

Cover photo © Shutterstock/Naci Yavuz
Illustrations by Gray Publishing and Cartoon Studio
Produced and typeset in 11/11.5pt Folio Light by Integra Software Services Pvt. Ltd., Pondicherry, India
Printed and bound by CPI Group (UK) Ltd, Croydon, CR0 4YY

A catalogue record for this title is available from the British Library

ISBN: 978 1 5104 2933 8

Contents

Preface

This is one of a series of six titles fully updated for the National 4 & 5 History courses to be assessed from 2018 onwards. Students should study three main sections in National 4 & 5 History, with a very wide selection of topics to choose from (five in the first two, ten in the third). The series covers two topics in each section.

The six titles in the series are:

- National 4 & 5 History: Migration and Empire 1830–1939
- National 4 & 5 History: The Era of the Great War 1900–1928
- National 4 & 5 History: The Atlantic Slave Trade 1770–1807
- National 4 & 5 History: Changing Britain 1760–1914
- National 4 & 5 History: Hitler and Nazi Germany 1919–1939
- National 4 & 5 History: Free at Last? Civil Rights in the USA 1918–1968

Each book contains comprehensive coverage of the four SQA key issue areas for National 5, as well as guidance and practice on Assignment writing and assessment procedures.

The Assignment: what you need to know

National 5

What is the Assignment for National 5?

The Assignment is written under exam conditions and then sent to the SQA to be marked. It counts for 20 marks out of a total of 100, so doing well in the Assignment can provide you with a very useful launchpad for overall success in the National 5 exam.

The Assignment has two stages:

- research (the gathering together of your findings and sources). This can be done at any appropriate point in the course.
- production of evidence (the writing up, in exam conditions, in the allotted one-hour sitting).

How should I write my Assignment?

You are given marks for showing certain skills in your Assignment. Firstly, you must choose a question to write about. That means your title should end with a question mark. Once your question is sorted, you must aim to:

- Write an introduction that sets the context for your question and which outlines different, relevant factors.
- Organise your information so that it makes sense as a balanced answer to your main question.

- Use your own knowledge and understanding to explain and analyse the question you have chosen.
- Use information gathered from *at least* two relevant sources to address and support these factors. For example, two books or one book plus an interview.
- Use other detailed information to support these.
- Evaluate which of the factors were more important than others.
- Identify and assess different perspectives and/or points of view (try to include *at least* two).
- Reach a conclusion that states what you think is the main answer to your question.
- Give reasons to support your conclusion.

What should I write about?

Here are some suggestions for suitable Assignment questions based on the content of this book:

✓ To what extent were cuts in the German military the biggest cause of German anger about the Treaty of Versailles?
✓ Is it true to say that the Weimar Republic tried to create a fair system of law and government?
✓ How important were economic problems as the main reason for the Weimar Republic's unpopularity between 1919 and 1933?
✓ How important was the role of Hitler in the rise to power of the Nazis?
✓ 'Although Hitler became Chancellor of Germany in 1933, he did not have complete power until August 1934.' How true is that statement?
✓ How important was fear in explaining Nazi power in Germany 1933–39?
✓ To what extent did Nazi social and economic policies create a 'feel-good factor' for most Germans between 1933 and 1939?

The following list contains examples of badly worded Assignment titles:

✗ The Treaty of Versailles.
✗ The Weimar Republic.
✗ The problems caused by hyperinflation.
✗ The Nazi rise to power.
✗ Nazi control of Germany.
✗ The Jews in Nazi Germany.

These are just headings, not questions. And because they are not structured as questions, they are too broad in scope and focus on areas that will not offer you the opportunity to gain maximum marks.

Be safe! There are no prizes for giving yourself a difficult question that you have made up yourself. Choose something from the history you have already been studying. You could choose a title from a past exam paper: www.sqa.org.uk/sqa/47447 or modify a past paper question, with help from your teacher. Avoid doing something risky – you only get one chance at this Assignment.

How long should my Assignment be?

Your Assignment has no word count limit – it all depends on how much you can write in the permitted hour. Most Assignments are about four or five pages long.

Remember that you also have a Resource Sheet to help you

On your Resource Sheet you will write out the sources that you will refer to in your Assignment. This will show the marker that you have researched, selected and organised your information.

Your Resource Sheet will be sent to the SQA with your finished Assignment. You will not be given a mark for your completed Resource Sheet, but markers will use it to see that you have done the necessary research and have found appropriate sources to use in your Assignment. The Resource Sheet is *yours*. You can change it, colour it or print it out. You can write it anywhere, anytime before you write your Assignment under exam conditions. You can include bullet points, spidergrams (spider diagrams), notes, names, dates. The only strict rules are that your Resource Sheet must:

- not be longer than 200 words
- be on one side of A4
- contain the title and author of *at least* two sources you are referring to in your Assignment.

You must **not** copy out large sections from your Resource Sheet into your Assignment, but you **can** copy across quotes from your sources that you have in your Resource Sheet.

National 4: Added Value Unit

The Assignment (sometimes called the Added Value Unit) lets you show off your skills as you research a historical issue. You have a lot of choice in what you can investigate and you can also choose to present your findings in different ways. That means you don't *have* to write an essay to display your skills, knowledge and understanding.

To be successful in National 4 you have to show that you can research and use information by doing the following things:

- Choosing an appropriate historical theme or event for study. Your teacher can help you choose.
- Collecting relevant evidence from *at least two* sources of information.
- Organising and using the information that you have collected to help you write about the subject you have chosen.
- Describing what your chosen subject is about.
- Explaining why your chosen subject happened (its cause) or explaining what happened next because of your chosen subject (its effects).

As you work through this book you will make mobiles, give presentations, and create posters, diagrams and artwork. All these things could be part of your National 4 Assignment. You then have to present your findings.

Don't worry – if you get stuck your teacher is allowed to give you help and advice at *any* stage as you do your Assignment.

Do I have to write a long essay?

No, you don't. You can choose how you present your Assignment. For example, you could give a talk and then be asked some questions about your subject by your teacher. You could do a PowerPoint presentation or keep a learning log. You might decide to design a poster or use some other way to display your work. But yes, you *could* write an essay if you wanted to!

1 Introduction

What is this course about?

This book is about changes in Germany between 1918 and 1939. The timeline shown here is meant to introduce new political words to you. It will help you by starting to sort out the changes that happened in Germany between 1918 and 1939 and also give some idea of when the changes took place.

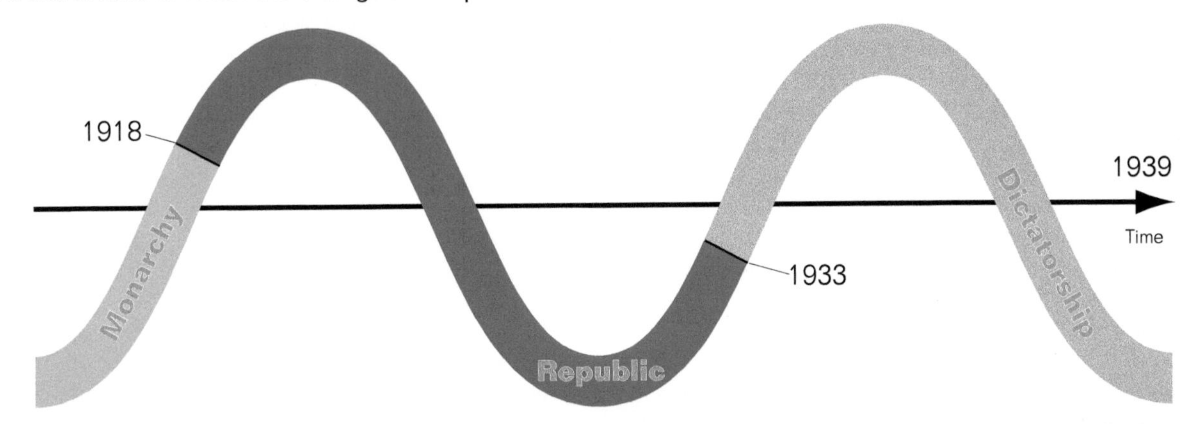

What will this book help me to do?

This book will help you to be successful in your National 4 and 5 History course. It contains everything you need to know about all the key issues and descriptions of content outlined by the SQA for 'Hitler and Nazi Germany 1919–1939'.

The book provides advice and examples to help you answer all the different types of questions you are likely to face in the National 5 exam.

Finally, this book will provide guidance to help you work on the Assignment tasks.

GLOSSARY

Monarchy a political system with a royal family at its head

Republic a political system with no royal family

Dictatorship a political system with one person or political party in total control and no opposition allowed

Activity 1

Timeline creation

Carefully draw your own version of the timeline shown on the previous page *or* you could make a very large version of the timeline and display it in your classroom. Or you could even do both!

The classroom timeline could be used to add important events or people as and when they appear in the story of Germany between 1918 and 1939.

Your criteria check

- Does your copy of the timeline use three different colours?
- Does your copy of the timeline cover the years 1918–1939?
- Does your copy of the timeline use different colours for the different political systems that ruled Germany between 1918 and 1939?
- Does your copy of the timeline have accurate labels naming the different political systems beside the colours?

Activity 2

True or false

In your workbook or work file write the heading: 'Germany 1918–1939'. Read the list of statements below and then write out the statements that you think are true based on what your timeline shows:

- There were three different political systems in Germany between 1918 and 1939.
- The monarchy was replaced by a dictatorship.
- The monarchy was replaced by a republic.
- A republic replaced a dictatorship.
- The republic was called a Nazi dictatorship.
- The republic was replaced by a dictatorship.
- Dictatorship followed on from a republic.
- The republic was a democracy.
- Dictatorship was a democracy.
- Monarchy was the same as a dictatorship.
- The Weimar Republic ended in 1918.
- In 1918 the monarchy ended in Germany.
- The monarchy was named Weimar.
- The Nazi republic started in 1933.
- There were three big political changes in Germany between 1918 and 1933.

Activity 3

Make your choices!

1. Choose which underlined word or phrase should be used in the following statements to make them correct.
2. Use your own sources of information, either classroom books or dictionaries or access to the internet, to help you make your choices.
3. Write a heading at the beginning of the list that best sums up what the list is about.
4. Write down the correct versions of the statements in your workbook or work file.

   - In 1918 the Kaiser abdicated and the monarchy ended/began.
   - A monarchy means a country not ruled/ruled by a royal family.
   - A republic means a country ruled/not ruled by a royal family.
   - A republic government is elected/not elected by the monarchy.
   - A republic government is elected/not elected by the adult people of the country.
   - A dictatorship means/does not mean one person and one political party only rules the country.
   - In a democracy people do/do not have many political choices.
   - In a dictatorship there are/are not political choices.

Now that you have completed the activities, you have an overall impression of what this course is about and the main changes that took place in Germany between the end of the First World War in 1918 and the beginning of the Second World War in 1939.

Now it is time to find out more detail.

2 Germany 1918

What is this chapter about?

Until November 1918, Germany was a monarchy led by a Kaiser. Kaiser Wilhelm II had been a popular leader, but by 1918 Germany was facing defeat in the First World War. The Kaiser was much less popular and in November 1918 he **abdicated** shortly before Germany surrendered. Germany was defeated and the German monarchy ended.

By the end of this chapter you should be able to:

- Describe the problems facing Germany at the end of the First World War.
- Explain why such big political changes happened in Germany at the end of the war.

How did the First World War affect Germany?

In 1914, **Kaiser** Wilhelm II led Germany. The Kaiser was a popular leader in Germany but countries such as Britain were suspicious about his true motives. Some of Germany's neighbours thought the Kaiser wanted war and was a threat to European peace.

The First World War started in 1914 and lasted until 1918. At first, all the countries involved believed they would win the war quite easily. A popular saying at the time was 'The war will be over by Christmas'. However, the war soon became bogged down in the stalemate of trench warfare. Nevertheless, soldiers and civilians on all sides were told that their country was winning.

GLOSSARY

Abdicated when the Kaiser gave up his power

Kaiser the emperor of Germany, Wilhelm II

Give three reasons to explain why you know this is *not* a German cartoon supporting the Kaiser.

An illustration of Kaiser Wilhelm II from about 1900 (left) and a cartoon 'He won't be happy till he gets it' showing the Kaiser in his bath from about 1914 (right)

Why was Germany facing such serious difficulties by 1918?

By the late summer of 1918, Germany was exhausted physically and emotionally. It was hard for Germans to continue to believe they were winning the war. The British naval blockade was hurting, effectively preventing all supplies getting into Germany. This meant that as the war went on, essential supplies of food, clothing, fuel, chemicals and medicines were harder and harder to find.

Coal was in seriously short supply, which led to widespread power cuts. Rationing reduced already scarce food supplies even further. People were reduced to searching in fields and gutters for scraps of rotting food. German citizens were desperate.

The people were starving, injured soldiers were having their wounds dressed in paper and many were deserting. When a flu epidemic swept through Germany, thousands died.

To make things worse, the USA had recently joined the war against Germany and in August 1918, a huge Allied offensive completely broke the German army's strength.

Do you agree that this drawing is effective in symbolising how many Germans felt by the end of the war?

This drawing shows a woman who has just been told her husband has been killed fighting, while her children are desperate for food

Why did the Kaiser have to abdicate?

German politicians hoped that if they could show that Germany was no longer led by the Kaiser and that it was creating a new democratic country, then Germany might not be so severely punished when it came to writing a peace treaty. That was why the *Reichstag* (the German Parliament) was given more power. A new political leader called Prince Max of Baden tried to make a deal with its enemies so that Germany would be treated fairly at the end of the war.

This is part of what Prince Max of Baden wrote to US President Wilson on 3 October 1918:

To avoid further bloodshed, the German government requests the President to bring about the immediate conclusion of an armistice, by land, by sea and in the air.

In early 1918, President Wilson had offered Germany a 14-point peace plan. At that time, the German military leaders had rejected Wilson's offer because they still expected to win the war. By November 1918, they could only hope to recover some of the peace terms previously offered by Wilson. However, when Prince Max asked President Wilson if his 14-point peace plan was still on offer, Wilson said no.

Although Wilson knew that a fair and reasonable peace treaty was the only thing that could secure future peace, by early November 1918 attitudes had hardened against Germany. The Allied leaders wanted to put the Kaiser on trial for war crimes and there was even a demand to 'Hang the Kaiser'. The Allies wanted to punish Germany and they made it clear that the Kaiser would have to go before they would stop the war.

Why did the war end in November 1918?

At the end of October 1918, discipline in the German navy cracked. The German commanders decided that the German navy should save its honour by sailing out into the North Sea for one last major battle with the British. The German sailors had different ideas. They did not want their lives and those of 80,000 others put at risk for a pointless battle. The word **mutiny** means when soldiers or sailors refuse to follow orders. That is exactly what happened at the German naval base of Kiel on 3 November 1918.

GLOSSARY

Mutiny when soldiers and sailors refuse to follow orders

The mutiny at Kiel sparked off other mutinies elsewhere, and by 6 November groups of soldiers, sailors and workers were in power in the ports of Hamburg, Bremen and Lübeck.

The soldiers, sailors and workers had formed 'workers' councils' to govern their local areas. They had copied their ideas from Russia where there had been a **revolution** a few months before. They even used the Russian word **soviet**, which means a local council. They also flew the red flag of revolution over their naval bases and towns. Soon the revolutionaries were called 'Reds'.

Jan Valtin, an eyewitness to the events of November 1918, wrote:

That night I saw the mutinous sailors roll in to Bremen in trucks – red flags and machine guns mounted on the trucks. Many of the workers were armed with guns, with bayonets, with hammers.

GLOSSARY

Revolution a big change in a political system, when the old system is completely overthrown, usually by violence

Soviet a local council made up of soldiers, sailors and workers to rule their own areas

The revolution spread quickly so that by 9 November, workers' and soldiers' councils even ruled in the capital city, Berlin.

Eventually, the Kaiser's closest advisers convinced him to give up the throne. On 9 November it was announced that the Kaiser would abdicate. On 10 November the Kaiser left Germany by train for the Netherlands, and on 11 November an armistice was signed. Germany was defeated, the war was lost.

Leaderless and beaten, revolutions broke out across the nation. What would happen to Germany now?

In what ways has the artist tried to illustrate the defeat of Germany?

A painting by Abel Faivre called l'Emprunt de la Libération ('the liberation loan')

Activity 1

Summarise this chapter

The following summary reminds you of what this chapter has been about. Words that are important in this chapter have been made into ANAGRAMS. Your task is to sort out the anagrams then write the correct version of this summary into your workbook or work file.

AIKRES Wilhelm **CATEDABDI** in November 1918, just before the armistice was signed. Germany was facing defeat in the First World War and **IONREVLOUT** broke out. When the German **ARCHYMON** ended, Germany became a **LICREPUB**.

Activity 2

If this is the answer what is the question?

Below you will find a list of words or names. You have to make up a question that can only be answered by the word on the list. For example, if the word 'Kaiser' was the answer, a question could be 'What was the title of the German leader up until 1918?'

Here is your list of answers:

- abdicated
- 9 November 1918
- an armistice
- a republic
- a monarchy
- 1914 until 1918
- President Wilson
- 14 points
- a mutiny
- the *Reichstag*.

Activity 3

The short challenge

Write a short summary of this chapter describing the main things that have happened. You must use *all* the words listed in Activity 2 in as few sentences as possible. Your title is: 'How did the First World War affect Germany?'

Question practice

National 4

The effects on Germany of the end of the First World War

The assessment is an oral (spoken) presentation. To pass this assessment, you will have to use Sources A–D and your own knowledge to design a presentation explaining the effects on Germany of the end of the First World War.

This could be a talk, speech, slide show, digital media production, video or any other appropriate method. You should:

- Explain the reasons why Germany lost the First World War.
- Explain why mutiny broke out in the navy and how the revolution spread.
- Describe the way that the monarchy ended in Germany.

Present your information clearly. A good quality presentation will help you demonstrate your skills and knowledge. Remember, you are being assessed only on your History and not your presentation abilities. Don't spend too much time on making things look wonderful.

The following sources are about the effects of the end of the First World War on Germany.

Source A is from a recent textbook about the end of the First World War.

SOURCE A

By autumn 1918 Germany was facing serious problems. The USA had recently joined the war against Germany and in August 1918, a huge Allied offensive completely broke the Germans' strength. By September, the Germans had lost one million soldiers, while the numbers of fresh, well-equipped US troops in Europe grew to over two million by the autumn of 1918.

Source B is from Jan Valtin, an eyewitness to the events of November 1918.

SOURCE B

Toward the end of October, 1918, my father wrote that the High Seas Fleet was under orders to go down in battle to save the honour of High Command. 'Their honour is not our honour', my father wrote. Then came stirring news. Mutiny in the Kaiser's fleet! Anxious voices cried out 'Will the fleet sail out! ... No, the fleet must not sail! It's murder! Finish the war!'

Source C is from an official announcement made by the German government.

SOURCE C

Monday, 11 November 1918: On Saturday the Kaiser abdicated the throne. The Imperial Chancellorship has been entrusted to the Socialist Herr Ebert. A decree signed by Prince Max promised a German National Assembly to settle finally the future form of government of the German nation.

Source D is from Jan Valtin, an eyewitness to the events of November 1918.

SOURCE D

That night I saw the mutinous sailors roll in to Bremen in caravans of commandeered trucks – red flags and machine guns mounted on the trucks. Many of the workers were armed with guns, with bayonets, with hammers. A frightened old woman wailed piercingly 'what is all this? What is the world coming to?' A young worker grasped the old woman's shoulders. He laughed resoundingly. 'Revolution', he rumbled. 'Revolution, Madam.'

Sources A, B, C and D all give evidence as to what happened in Germany at the end of the war.

Draw a diagram showing what took place in Germany in late 1918. You might decide to draw a series of footprints or a staircase diagram, with steps going up in a diagonal line. By using sources A, B, C and D in that order, at each stage of your diagram write one main thing that occurred in Germany in the last months of 1918.

National 5

Here are two examples of typical 'Evaluate the usefulness' questions that you might be asked at National 5.

Source A is from the memories of Greta Haffner, a German woman whose husband had been killed in the First World War.

SOURCE A

Although November 1918 meant the end of the war, I recall no sense of joy. There was only confusion as men returned from the Front. On Saturday, the papers announced the Kaiser's abdication. On Sunday, I heard shots fired in the streets of Berlin. During the whole war I hadn't heard a single shot, yet now the war was over they began shooting. I felt uneasy. On November 11th, I saw the newspaper headline 'Armistice Signed'. I turned to stone. I felt my whole world had collapsed.

1 Evaluate the usefulness of Source A as evidence of attitudes of Germans towards the end of the First World War. **(5 marks)**

'Evaluate' means to judge or weigh up the usefulness of a source as evidence for (or against) something. When answering this type of question, it is never enough just to describe what is in a source and you can gain marks in three different ways.

The first is to write about *who* wrote it, *when* and *why* it was written and to EXPLAIN WHY that information makes the source *more* or *less useful.* That's worth up to 4 marks.

For example, you could write, 'This source is useful as evidence because it is directly relevant to the question. The source was written by a German woman whose husband has been killed. This is useful as evidence because she is an eyewitness to events and she records how her world is now confusing and dangerous because of Germany's surrender.'

The second way is to focus on what is useful IN the source, in terms of what the question is asking. That is worth up to 2 marks. You need to find evidence from the source AND make a comment about how useful the evidence is for 1 mark. You can make up to two points and gain a maximum of 2 marks for this.

The third method is to write about what makes the source less than useful. Think about what could have been included which would have made the source more useful as evidence in terms of the question. This is worth up to 2 marks.

Source B was written by Max Brubeck, a soldier in the trenches when the armistice was announced in November 1918.

SOURCE B

At first we could not believe it. Could the war really be over? At first we were happy and relieved – we had lived through this terrible war but then it hit us – we had lost! How was it possible? We were stunned, shocked and then angry. Only a few short weeks before we were told we were winning this war. Our forces were advancing forward. Our enemies were starving at home. Now we realised it was all lies. Who had done this to us? Who had stabbed us in the back? Our Kaiser has let us down – he must hang his head in disgrace.

2 Evaluate the usefulness of Source B as evidence of attitudes of Germans towards the end of the First World War. **(5 marks)**

Use the advice given above on how to answer question 1, to write your own answer to this question.

SECTION 1

Weimar Germany 1919–1929

3 The Spartacists

What is this chapter about?

When the Kaiser abdicated, a new **Provisional Government** was formed (provisional means temporary). It was led by Friedrich Ebert, leader of the Social Democratic Party (SPD). Germany also became a republic, which is a form of government where elected representatives run the country without a royal family having any political influence. Ebert knew there were groups in Germany who did not want the new Provisional Government to be successful. One of these groups was the Spartacists, who later became known as the Communist Party (or KPD for short). Ebert used groups of ex-soldiers called *Freikorps* to destroy the Spartacists.

By the end of this chapter you should be able to:

- Explain why the Spartacists wanted to overthrow Ebert's government.
- Describe how the Spartacist rising was crushed.

Why was Ebert against revolution?

Friedrich Ebert believed that revolutionary groups such as the **Spartacists** would destroy Germany. Ebert wanted to create a democratic Germany where people would elect representatives who would work in the *Reichstag* to pass laws to help the German people. Ebert was looking for a Parliament that was similar to Britain's in which people with different opinions argued for their point of view. Ebert was leader of the SPD – the Social Democratic Party – but he believed there should be many other political parties representing the views of all sections of Germany's population. Ebert also knew that these political changes would take time to become established in Germany but time was something Ebert did not have. Revolutionary groups wanted immediate changes in Germany.

Ebert feared the spread of a revolution that would perhaps result in only one political party – the Communists – dominating Germany. That was why Ebert was against the Spartacists.

GLOSSARY

Provisional Government a temporary government created until full elections could take place

Friedrich Ebert leader of the Social Democratic Party and head of the Provisional Government

Spartacists revolutionaries who wanted to make Germany into a Communist state

What did the Spartacists want?

The Spartacists were Communists who wanted a revolution similar to the one in Russia in 1917.

Spartacists wanted a new type of government that ruled on behalf of the poor and powerless in Germany. The Spartacists believed that power should be in the hands of the workers' and soldiers' councils that had sprung up at the end of the war. The Spartacists certainly did not want to work with a parliamentary system with long discussions and only slow change. In fact, one of the Spartacist demands was 'Abolish all parliaments and transfer all power to the workers' and soldiers' councils!'

The Spartacists argued that if change did not happen quickly then the powerful groups in society would use their power to stop real change in Germany and the revolution that had started at the end of the war would fail.

It was clear that there was little chance of agreement between Ebert and the Spartacists. The scene was set for conflict between the more democratic 'slow change' ideas of Ebert and the revolutionary 'fast change' ideas of the Spartacists.

What are the similarities between the poster and the aims of the Spartacists?

The Spartacists believed that power should be taken away from the businessmen, the high-ranking army officers and the wealthy sections of German society. The picture is of a Russian communist poster from 1918.

How did Ebert prepare for the Spartacist challenge?

Ebert knew that the Spartacists were getting ready for an armed uprising, so he was aware that he would have to meet force with force. Ebert asked the army for support but the officers in the army were less than happy to help. During the war, Ebert had often criticised the war and the Kaiser. However, the army leaders hated the idea of a Spartacist revolution more than they disliked Ebert so on 10 November 1918 (that's even before the armistice!) Ebert did a deal with General Groener, chief of the German army.

Ebert promised to do nothing to harm the interests of the army if Groener and his troops would defend Ebert's government against the revolutionary Spartacists.

General Groener wrote in his diary, '... we worked out a programme for cleaning up Berlin and the disarming of the Spartacists'. Ebert also asked his new minister for defence – called Gustav Noske – to organise volunteer units of loyal ex-soldiers who would be willing to fight the Spartacists. They were called the ***Freikorps***.

GLOSSARY

Freikorps battle-hardened ex-soldiers who hated Communists or Spartacists

Why did the *Freikorps* hate the Spartacists?

The *Freikorps* were groups of volunteer ex-soldiers, most of them experienced, battle-hardened and heavily armed. They also believed that Germany had lost the war because they had been betrayed – or stabbed in the back – by revolutionaries such as the Spartacists. The *Freikorps* blamed the Spartacists for the humiliation of defeat.

Ebert also feared that the Spartacists might get help from Communist Russia and at first the *Freikorps* were recruited to protect Germany in case of Communist attack from Russia. As it happened, Russia did not try to help the Spartacists but the *Freikorps* were ready for a fight.

What happened when the Spartacists tried to start a revolution?

In January 1919, there was a large demonstration of about 100,000 workers in Berlin. Times were hard, the naval blockade was still causing huge problems in Germany and thousands of people were starving and unemployed. The Spartacists hoped these people could be turned into a revolutionary force and fight for their revolution. Unfortunately for the Spartacists, they had not really planned how to do that.

Spartacist supporters did take over the centre of Berlin but there were no clear plans about how to proceed. While Spartacist leaders spent hours discussing what to do next, armed workers stood aimlessly in the freezing streets. Many of them gave up and went home. Then the *Freikorps* arrived with machine guns on armoured cars painted with skulls and crossbones and began shooting.

Within one week – known as Bloody Week – the attempted revolution ended in a sea of blood on the streets of Berlin. Almost 700 'revolutionaries' were captured and executed by the *Freikorps*. When the leaders of the Spartacists, Karl Liebknecht and Rosa Luxemburg, were arrested they never went to trial. Liebknecht was shot, 'while trying to escape' and Rosa Luxemburg's dead body was dumped in a canal.

Why do you think this image was drawn and how would it affect members of the *Freikorps*?

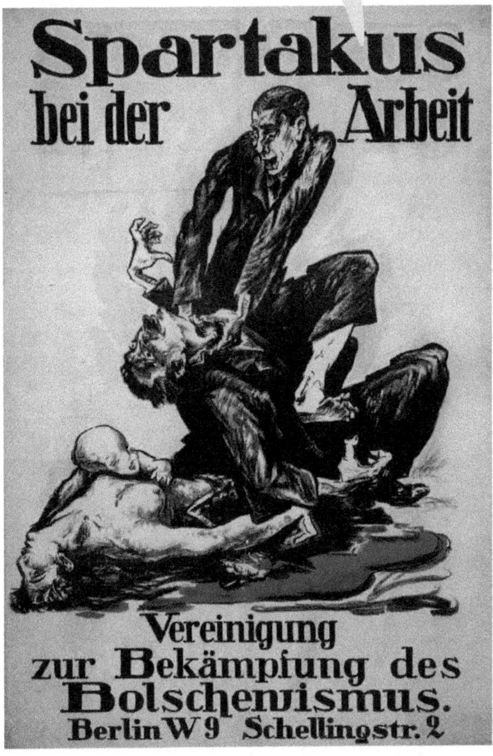

A German political poster from 1919, 'Spartakus at work', showing a member of the Spartacists murdering a family

The Freikorps were equipped with flame-throwers

What does this picture tell us about why the Spartacist rising was doomed to fail?

What did the Spartacist rising have to do with the rise of Hitler over 10 years later?

The answer is quite a lot. Both Ebert's SPD party and the Spartacists (later called the KPD) were **left-wing** parties. They both wanted power for the people of Germany. They just disagreed about how to get and use that power.

Ten years later, Hitler would come to power. Hitler and the Nazis were **right wing**, the opposite of the SPD and the KPD.

GLOSSARY

Left wing people who wanted revolution and power to the working classes

Right wing people who did not want change and, in fact, wanted power to go back to the Kaiser and the upper classes

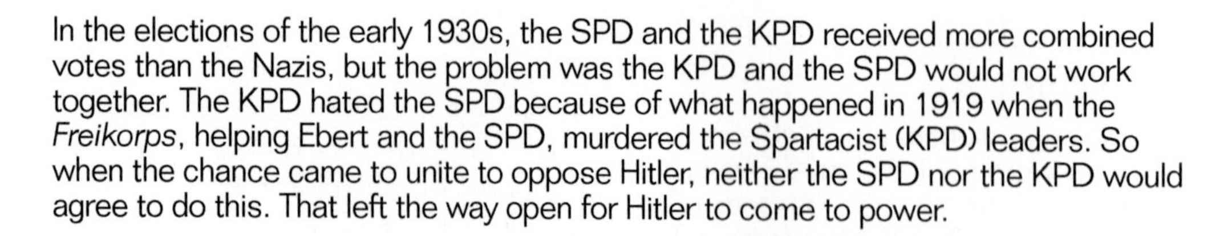

In the elections of the early 1930s, the SPD and the KPD received more combined votes than the Nazis, but the problem was the KPD and the SPD would not work together. The KPD hated the SPD because of what happened in 1919 when the *Freikorps*, helping Ebert and the SPD, murdered the Spartacist (KPD) leaders. So when the chance came to unite to oppose Hitler, neither the SPD nor the KPD would agree to do this. That left the way open for Hitler to come to power.

Activity 1

Summarise this chapter

The following summary reminds you of what this chapter has been about. Words that are important in this chapter have been made into ANAGRAMS. Your task is to sort out the anagrams then write the correct version of this summary into your workbook or work file.

Germany had a **ISIONALPROV** government when the war ended. It was led by **TEREB**, who was worried that the **TACISTSSPAR** would start a violent **UTIONREVOL**. Ebert made a deal with ex-soldiers called the **ORPSFREIK** who were used to **YTRODES** the Spartacists.

Activity 2

Describe the aims of the Spartacists

Select a word or phrase to fill in the missing parts shown by the numbers in the summary below. Once you have decided what goes where, write out the whole summary under the heading 'What did the Spartacists want?' into your workbook or work file.

The Spartacists were led by [1]. They wanted to [2] the wealth of the rich people. With so many Germans starving, they wanted a government which [3]. In 1917 the Bolsheviks in Russia had shown that a small group of [4] could overthrow a government. The Spartacists wanted to copy [5] by having their own [6] in Germany.

a take away
b revolution
c ruled on behalf of the poor
d Karl Liebknecht and Rosa Luxemburg
e the Russian example
f Communists

Activity 3

The challenge! How far can you go?

The following questions go up in levels of difficulty in pairs. The first two are easy. The last two are hard. How many will you try to do?

1 Can you suggest another word for revolution?
2 Why did the Spartacists try to start a revolution?

3 Can you explain what the phrase Provisional Government means?
4 How would you summarise the attitudes of the *Freikorps* towards the Spartacists?

5 Just by looking at the pictures of the fighting in Berlin, what conclusions can you make about who was likely to win the struggle and why?
6 If you had been a member of the Spartacists, how would you have improved their chances of success?

Activity 4

Here is a cartoon drawn at the time of the Spartacist revolt.

It tries to show what the Spartacists wanted. You can see a Spartacist fighting against a multi-headed monster. The Spartacist is trying to cut off the heads of things he does not like. Some of the heads have been cut off, but there are some still to be defeated.

Your task is to use the internet to search for a different picture, photograph or cartoon about the Spartacist rising.

- Go to Google Images™ and type 'Spartacists, Berlin 1919'.
- Select an image and either print it out and stick in your workbook or paste it into your electronic file.
- Try to write five comments about why you chose it and what the picture tells you about the Spartacist revolt.

4 The new constitution

What is this chapter about?

The German political system between the end of 1918 and 1933 was called the Weimar Republic. Weimar is the name of the town where the rules about how the new republic would operate, called a constitution, were created. The Weimar constitution was meant to create a fair and democratic Germany.

By the end of this chapter you should be able to:

- Describe how the new German constitution was meant to be fair for everyone.
- Explain why the new Weimar Republic was not welcomed by all.

Why was the new republic named after the town of Weimar?

Suppose a revolution broke out in the streets near the Scottish Parliament in Edinburgh. Suppose there was fighting in the streets and people were being killed. It's not likely that the Scottish politicians would want to keep meeting in the middle of Edinburgh. They would want to go somewhere where they felt safe and could carry on without the threat of violence. That is exactly what happened in Germany. With violence in the streets of Berlin, the new German government moved to the quiet, peaceful town of **Weimar** until peace returned to Berlin.

GLOSSARY

Weimar a town in central Germany

National Assembly the name of the Parliament in the Weimar Republic

Constitution a set of rules for running a country

The new Parliament of the republic was called a **National Assembly**. It was elected by all German men and women over the age of 20. That was very democratic, even compared to Britain. At that time only men over the age 21 and some women over 30 could vote in Britain. The politicians who met at Weimar wanted to make sure the new political system would be fair to all people. To do that, the National Assembly had to create a new **constitution**. A constitution is a set of rules and principles on how people in a country will be governed and treated by the law.

Do you think the two pictures show the reasons why the new German government went to Weimar?

Tanks accompanied by government troops on the way to protect the police headquarters in Berlin in 1919

A postcard of a country house in Weimar in 1920

Was the constitution of the new Weimar Republic as fair and democratic as it was claimed to be?

Here are some ideas to suggest that the new constitution did *try* to be fair but did not always achieve what it set out to do.

Yes, it was

The new rules in the constitution were called articles and Article 125 stated that the politicians elected to represent the people in the National Assembly would be elected in secret by men and women over 20 years of age.

Not sure

The head of the German state was the president and he was to be elected once every seven years – but only by people over 35 years of age. The idea was to only allow people who were less likely to be revolutionary to vote.

Yes, it was

The German Parliament was called the *Reichstag*. The *Reichstag* had the power to remove important politicians such as chancellors (a bit like our prime minister) and cabinet ministers (politicians in charge of large government departments). The people of Germany elected members of the *Reichstag*.

Maybe not

Chancellors and cabinet ministers were given their jobs by the president.

Yes, it was

The voting system was fair. It used **proportional representation** (PR) which meant political parties gained a number of representatives in the *Reichstag* based on the share of votes that party got at the election. Even small parties that did not win many votes still won a voice in the *Reichstag*.

> **GLOSSARY**
>
> **Proportional representation** a voting system that assigns seats in proportion to the votes cast
>
> **Article 48** a law allowing the president to rule Germany in an emergency

No, it was not

Article 48 of the constitution gave the president powers to rule Germany directly, even by force, if there was an emergency. Article 48 stated clearly that in an emergency the president '... may suspend for the time being, the fundamental rights of the people'. The idea of Article 48 seemed sensible in 1919 when there were threats of emergencies caused by revolutionaries. But what would happen if a person who wanted to destroy the republic gained influence over the president? Later, you will find out how Hitler gained control of the president and used Article 48 to destroy the democratic Weimar Republic.

Yes, it was

When the Republic began, all citizens of Germany were given basic civil rights which meant they would be treated fairly. These rights were called the Fundamental Laws.

The box below shows some of the Fundamental Laws.

> You will need these articles for Activity 3 and you will need a dictionary!

Article 109 All Germans are equal before the law.

Article 114 Personal freedom is inviolable. No restraint or deprivation of personal liberty by the public power is admissible, unless authorised by law.

Article 115 The residence of every German is a sanctuary for him and inviolable.

Article 116 No one may be punished for an act unless such act was legally punishable at the time when it was committed.

Article 117 The secrecy of correspondence, as well as the secrecy of postal and telephonic communications is inviolable.

Article 118 Every German is entitled within the limits of the general law freely to express his opinions by word of mouth, writing, printing, pictorial representation, or otherwise. Laws are also permitted for the purpose of combating pornographic publications.

Article 124 All Germans have the right to form societies or associations for any object that does not run counter to the criminal law ... The same provisions apply to religious societies and bodies.

How did many Germans feel about their new government?

Perhaps the new constitution tried to be too fair. Some people at the time called the new republic '... the most perfect democracy on paper'. That means it looked good but in reality there were problems. What were those problems?

The voting system created problems

The PR voting system was fair but also confusing to people who were not used to voting at elections. PR never produced one clear winner and governments were always **coalitions**, which meant different parties shared power so people never got the party policies they voted for.

Even the party that won most seats in the *Reichstag* could be outnumbered by other parties joining together to outvote it.

GLOSSARY

Coalitions political parties working together to form a government

The fair system gave its enemies respectability

Even small parties with some votes were entitled to a few politicians in the *Reichstag*. The crazy thing was that political parties such as the Communists and Nazis eventually all sat in the *Reichstag* when what they really wanted to do was to destroy the *Reichstag* and German democracy.

What is this cartoon saying about the problems of the new Weimar constitution? In a democracy should all political parties and opinions be allowed a voice – even if their ideas are undemocratic?

Most Germans just did not like the new government

Many important Germans remained loyal to the 'Old Germany' and did not see why the government should be handed over to people who they thought of as incapable of governing.

Many German army officers claimed that Germany had lost the war because of the revolutionaries who mutinied and refused to follow orders. These people believed that Germany had been 'stabbed in the back' by enemies inside Germany such as the socialists in the SPD.

Many of the working classes who had supported revolution did not like the new system that allowed the wealthier classes to keep much of their power.

Even Germans who welcomed democracy were left discontented. The voting system was confusing. The results of elections were confusing also. New coalition governments seemed to change almost every month. There was little stability.

Many Germans looked back on the 'good old days' when the Kaiser was in charge and ordinary Germans did not have hard political choices to make.

This cartoon shows a horse with Ebert's head being forced to react to violence from the two figures on its back

Democracy was linked to defeat

In June 1919, Germany signed the Treaty of Versailles. The new Weimar government had no choice but many Germans blamed the government for the humiliation that came with the treaty. Many Germans linked the new government with defeat and humiliation. There was a loss of confidence in the new republic.

Signing the Treaty of Versailles marked the end of the First World War. This will be discussed in more detail in the next chapter.

To summarise, the fair and democratic republic did not start with many friends. Then things got worse.

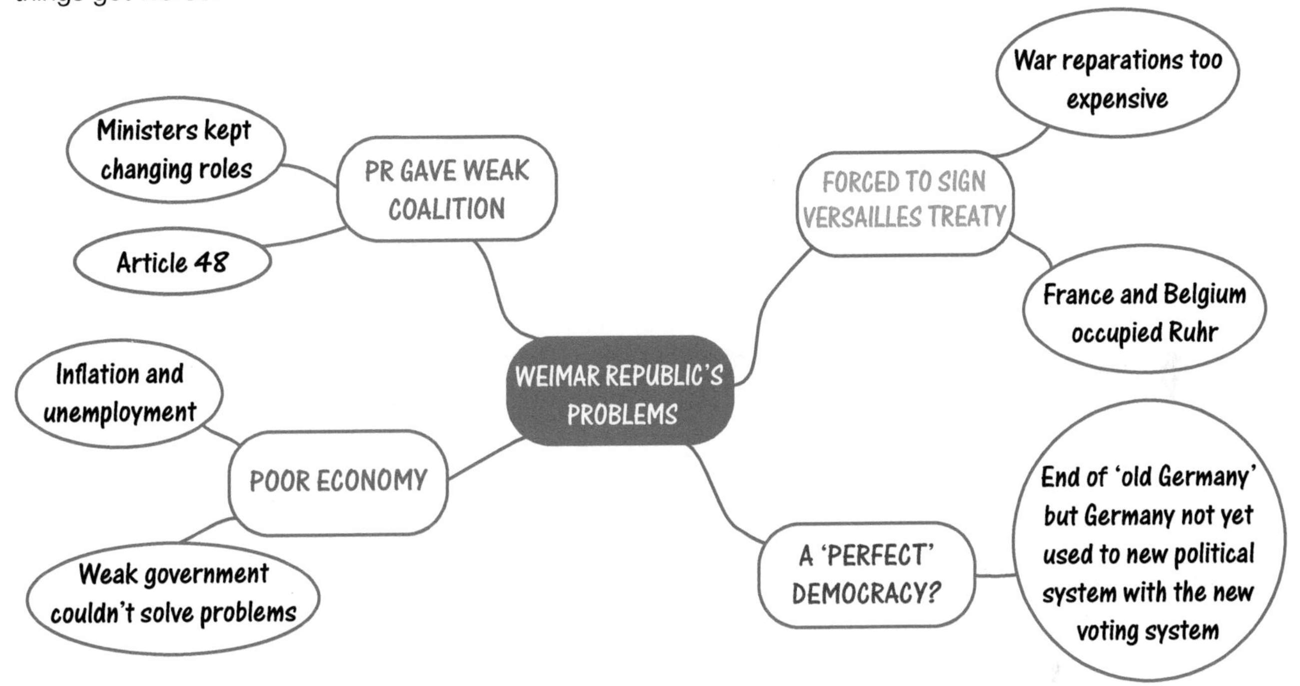

The above spidergram shows the problems faced by the new Weimar government. This is something that could help you to revise effectively, so think about trying this method in other chapters.

Activity 1

Summarise this chapter

The following summary reminds you of what this chapter has been about. Words that are important in this chapter have been made into ANAGRAMS. Your task is to sort out the anagrams then write the correct version of this summary into your workbook or work file.

The new **LICREPUB** was named after the town of **REIMAW**. The new **STITUCONTOIN** of Germany was designed to be very **ARIF**. The new voting system resulted in a series of very weak **TILCOANOI** governments. Many Germans did not like the new Weimar Republic.

Activity 2

If this is the answer what is the question?

Below you will find a list of words or names. You have to make up a question that could only be answered by the word on the list. For example, if the word 'Weimar' was the answer, a question could be 'Where was the new German constitution written?'

Here is your list of answers:

- constitution
- republic
- articles
- Fundamental Laws
- Weimar (use a different question than the example above!)
- 20
- 48
- 35
- PR.

Activity 3

Your challenge is to design a display that shows clearly and memorably why the Weimar constitution is still thought to be a real attempt at creating a fair society.

Why do this? Later in this book you will look at the laws introduced by the Nazis. They deliberately destroyed the basic rights given to people in the Weimar constitution. You will be able to see clearly the contrast between Weimar democracy and Nazi dictatorship.

Work in pairs. As a class, decide which pair is focusing on which article of the constitution.

Success criteria

- Your display must combine a graphic with words.
- Each pair must first of all work out what their article really means.
- Then think how that article would help to create a fairer society.
- Use a dictionary or ask for advice if necessary.
- Agree with your partner on a sentence which rewrites the meaning of each article in a form of words you understand.
- Plan a graphic or cartoon which illustrates exactly the point made by each article.
- Remember to be respectful of the work of others.
- Use your phones or tablets to take photos of all the displays.

You can now put all the photos into a folder entitled 'The Weimar constitution: a fair democracy'. You now have a classroom display and also an effective revision tool sharing everyone's work.

Question practice

National 4

Source A is written by a modern historian.

SOURCE A

The new constitution is to be welcomed. For the first time the ordinary people have a political voice that really counts. They are also free to vote and free to have their own opinions. But they have duties, especially the duty to guard against extremists who will want to destroy this 'perfect democracy'.

Describe in your own words why the writer thought Germans should welcome the new constitution. You should use Source A and your own knowledge.

Success criteria

Write at least two factual points of information, or one developed piece of information, on how Germans felt about the new constitution.

National 5

This is a 'how fully' question. In this type of question you need to select the points from the source which are relevant to the question – usually there will be three points in the source. Then, to get full marks you need to bring in points from recall that are also relevant to the question which are not mentioned in the source. Finally, You MUST make a judgement about the fullness (or completeness) of the source as an explanation, otherwise you can only achieve a maximum of 2 marks.

Source A explains the weakness of governments during the Weimar Republic.

SOURCE A

For many years the largest party, the SPD, refused to join any coalition. This meant that all governments had the support of less than half the members of the Reichstag which made it difficult to rule the country. The result was that coalitions kept being defeated and new governments had to be formed. There were six different coalition governments which tried to run Germany between 1923 and 1928. The longest lasted just 21 months.

How fully does Source A explain the reasons for the weakness of the government in Germany during the Weimar Republic. (6 marks)

Here is an example of a not very good answer:

The source partly explains the reasons for the weakness of the government. It points out that the largest party during the Weimar Republic, the SPD, refused to join any coalition government. The SPD decided not to share power with the other parties which had done well in the election. This meant that the coalitions kept being defeated and new governments were constantly being formed. What happened was that whenever a government collapsed a new one had to be formed. The source points out that there were six different coalitions with the longest lasting 21 months. This means that governments were changing every 3.5 months.

This is a weak answer because it includes three points from the source but there is no recall so it only gets 3 out of 6 marks. Can you write a better answer?

5 The Treaty of Versailles

What is this chapter about?

On 28 June 1919 Germany signed the Treaty of Versailles. The treaty officially ended the First World War. German politicians had hoped that since their country was now a democratic republic, they would have a say in negotiating a fair treaty. They were wrong. In the treaty, Germany was not only punished, it was humiliated. The German representatives were told to sign the treaty without discussion or the war would start again. Germany had no choice but to accept the peace terms. However, that did not stop many Germans from blaming their new democratic republic for signing the treaty.

By the end of this chapter you should be able to:

- Describe the main terms of the Treaty of Versailles.
- Explain why so many Germans hated the treaty.

What were the main terms of the Treaty of Versailles?

The victorious Allies wanted to make sure that Germany would never be a threat to European peace again. The first aim of the Treaty of **Versailles** was to make Germany a much weaker country.

German military might was drastically reduced:

- German army cut to 100,000 men.
- German navy cut to six warships.
- German weapons of war melted down for scrap metal.

Germany was banned from:

- having conscription
- having submarines
- having an air force
- having any tanks
- making an alliance with Austria
- having any soldiers or military equipment in the Rhineland, an area of western Germany beside the Dutch, Belgian and French borders with Germany.

Germany also had to give away part of its territory:

- Land was given to Belgium, France, Denmark and Poland.
- All German colonies were given away, many to Britain.
- Germany was split into two parts. The Allies thought that the old core of military Germany was a German state called Prussia so East Prussia was split off from the rest of Germany. East Prussia was separated from the rest of Germany by the 'Polish Corridor', a big strip of land given to the new country of Poland.

And still it was not enough. Germany was forced to accept responsibility for causing *all* the deaths and damage done during the war. That part of the treaty was called the **war guilt** clause. Of course, once Germany had 'accepted' it was guilty of causing the war, it was only natural to insist that Germany paid compensation to the Allies as a result! The word used for this compensation was **reparations**.

GLOSSARY

Versailles a palace near Paris where the peace treaty ending the First World War was signed

War guilt part of the Treaty of Versailles which claimed that Germany had caused the war and so was also to blame for all the death and destruction it produced

Reparations compensation that Germany had to pay for causing the war

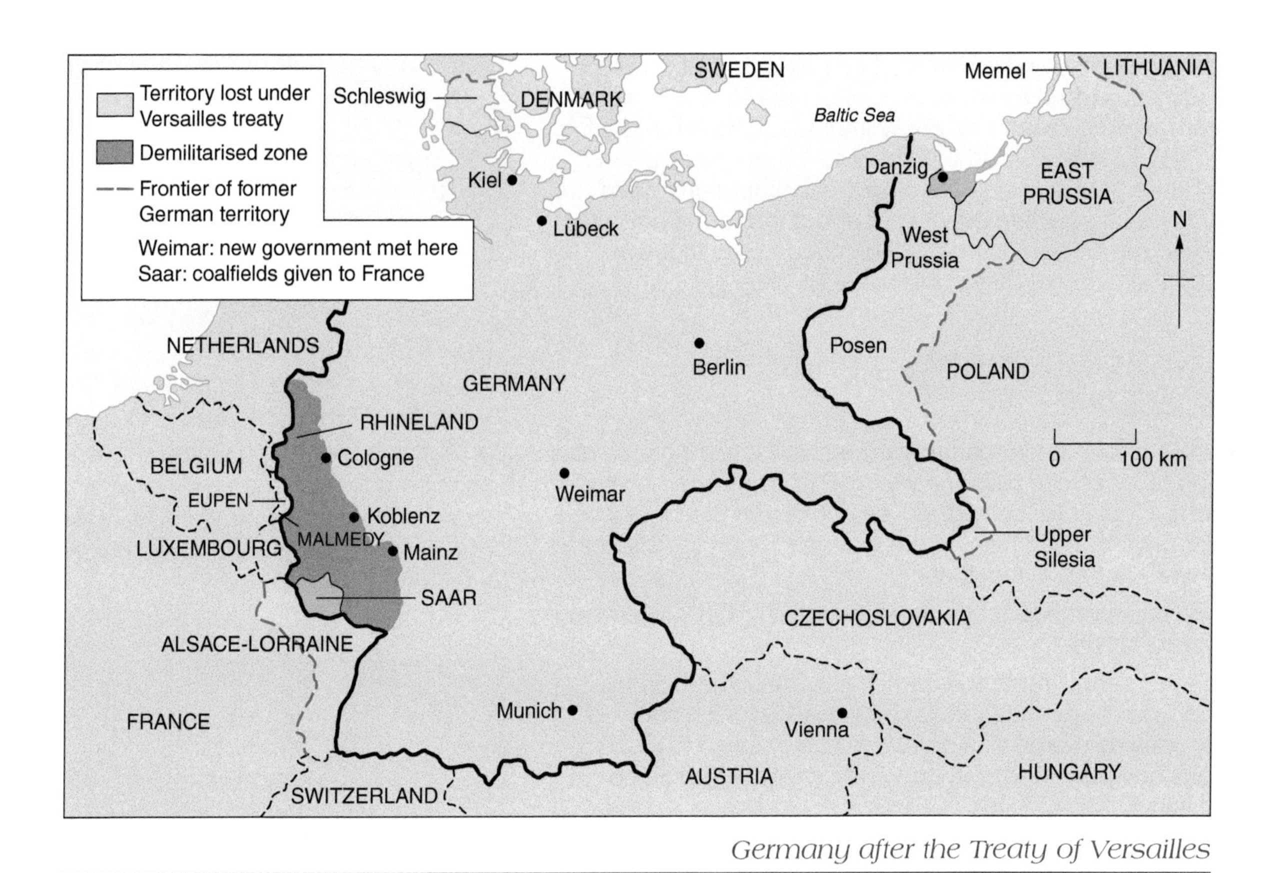

Germany after the Treaty of Versailles

Why were so many Germans angry about the treaty?

Some German military commanders wanted to continue the war even though it was hopeless. They thought it better to die honourably rather than accept a disgraceful treaty.

Many Germans believed that Germany had not really been defeated. They asserted, rightly, that Germany had not been invaded and claimed that Germany had been 'sold out' by the politicians who accepted the armistice on 11 November 1918. Those politicians were nicknamed the 'November Criminals'.

There was a belief that the German army had been weakened by revolutionaries back home who mutinied and would not follow orders. Those people who, it was said, had betrayed Germany were described as having 'stabbed Germany in the back'.

Why are myths more important than facts sometimes?

GLOSSARY

Stabbed in the back betrayed; some Germans felt they had lost the war because they had been stabbed in the back by revolutionaries back home

The stabbed in the back myth – the Dolchstoss – was a very powerful idea in 1920s' Germany. It suggested the German army had not been defeated but had been betrayed. In reality, Germany had lost the war because it ran out of resources and could not continue against an enemy that was reinforced by the USA.

The German people and politicians had believed that once the Kaiser abdicated, and a new democratic republic was created, then there was no reason why they should not be offered a fair treaty. This fair treaty would then help to rebuild Europe and secure future peace. Instead of a fair treaty, Germans were shocked and angry when they heard about the terms offered. They called the treaty a **diktat** – a dictated treaty that was forced on them. Were they right to feel so bitter?

GLOSSARY

Diktat linked to the English word 'dictated', it means Germans felt the treaty was forced on them, with no chance to discuss it

Why was the treaty so harsh on Germany?

When US President Wilson had offered his 14-point peace plan based on fairness and justice early in 1918, the Germans had rejected it. Could Germany really expect to turn the clock back now that the USA had many more war dead and the American people were not so sympathetic?

When Russia surrendered to Germany in early 1918, Germany hammered Russia.

For four years the British and French population had been exposed to endless anti-German propaganda which showed the Germans as murderous monsters and worse. How could politicians now say to their voters that Germany should be treated fairly?

Do you agree with this view of the Allies who created the Treaty of Versailles? How can you tell this is probably a German painting? This cartoon has a very biased point of view. Should cartoons that only take one side in an argument be allowed in a democratic society?

Greed, revenge and other devils gloat over the Treaty of Versailles. This cartoon was drawn in 1919.

Were Germans right to blame the new republic for accepting the treaty?

Regardless of the truth about Germany's defeat and exhaustion in 1918, many Germans continued to link the republic with defeat and humiliation. The Versailles treaty played an important part in explaining why many people distrusted the new democratic government.

On the same day the treaty was signed a German newspaper printed this:

Vengeance!

Today at Versailles a disgraceful treaty is being signed. Never forget it!

Today German honour is dragged to the grave. Never forget it!

The German people will push forward to regain their pride.

We will have revenge for the shame of 1919!

Only a few people were realistic and realised that Germany had no choice but to sign the treaty. In her book *The Autobiography of a German Rebel* (Routledge, 1940), Toni Sender wrote:

What could we do? What was the alternative of not signing? The German people wanted peace, they were exhausted. Not to sign would mean occupation of the most important territories, the blockade continued, unemployment, hunger, the death of thousands, the holding back of our war prisoners – a catastrophe which would force us to sign more humiliating conditions.

What were the long-term effects of the Versailles treaty on Germany?

Within a few years Germany faced serious economic problems directly linked to the terms of the Treaty of Versailles.

A more dangerous outcome of the Treaty of Versailles was the way that Hitler used it in his rise to power. Over and over again Hitler blamed the 'November Criminals' who had 'stabbed Germany in the back'. Hitler used the sense of unfairness about Versailles to attract support. One of his big vote-catching promises was to destroy the Treaty of Versailles. As Hitler said, 'I will make Germany great again, but before that happens the Treaty of Versailles must be destroyed.'

Activity 1

Summarise this chapter

The following summary reminds you of what this chapter has been about. Words that are important in this chapter have been made into ANAGRAMS. Your task is to sort out the anagrams then write the correct version of this summary into your workbook or work file.

The **ATYTRE** *of* **VAILLESERS** *punished Germany for* **TINGSART** *the war. The Germans called it a* **TATKID** *peace because they had no say in deciding what was to happen. The German population was* **RYGNA** *when they heard how Germany was to be* **SHEDINUP**. *The new* **LICREBUP** *was blamed for accepting and signing the treaty.*

Activity 2

In this cartoon, Germany is being squeezed until it gasps for air and then the victorious Allies force the terms of the peace treaty down its throat 'whether you like it or not'. In other words it makes comments about the diktat nature of the treaty. Draw a sketch version of the cartoon and stick your copy in your workbook or include it in your electronic files. Now annotate the cartoon by drawing labels that point to the following features.

- Germany being squeezed.
- The peace terms that Germany is being forced to accept.
- Words in the cartoon that show a complete lack of sympathy for Germany.
- The Allies who are forcing Germany to accept the treaty.

Activity 3

Now draw your own annotated sketch cartoon or graphic that shows three things:

- some of the terms of the Treaty of Versailles
- the reaction of the German population
- how you (as the cartoonist) feel about the Treaty of Versailles.

Question practice

National 4

Source A is from a German newspaper of 28 June 1919.

SOURCE A

Vengeance!

Today at Versailles a disgraceful treaty is being signed. Never forget it!

Today German honour is dragged to the grave. Never forget it!

The German people will push forward to regain their pride.

We will have revenge for the shame of 1919!

Give reasons to explain the effect of the Treaty of Versailles on Germany. You should use Source A and your own knowledge.

Success criteria

Include at least two pieces of information explaining the effect of the peace treaty on Germany.

National 5

This is a comparison question. Comparison questions are easy to spot because they are the only ones that will refer to *two* sources.

Source A is part of a speech made in 1918 by Sir Eric Geddes, a representative of the British government.

SOURCE A

How should we deal with Germany? I can understand why the French want revenge. I personally think that we should get everything out of Germany that we can and perhaps a bit more – like squeezing out a lemon. I suggest that not only all the gold Germany has, but all the silver and jewels she has, should be handed over. Think of all our sacrifices. This is what they truly deserve.

Source B is based on a speech by President Wilson of the USA.

SOURCE B

The American people entered the war against Germany to create a world safe for democracy. This will not be achieved by punishing Germany and leaving the Germans angry and bitter. We must deal with Germany fairly to secure a safe future for everyone. France is wrong to search only for revenge.

Compare the opinions in Sources A and B about how Germany should be treated at the end of the First World War. **(4 marks)**

There are 4 marks for this question.

For this type of question you must make clear whether you think the sources agree or not.

In your exam you will get two comparison questions in total. One of them will have two sources that agree on a topic and the other question will have two sources that disagree.

For this question you would probably decide that the two sources disagree.

You must write *why* you think the sources disagree. This means you should quote a brief extract from the first source and choose another extract from the second source that makes an opposite point.

You will get 1 mark for each comparison if you just explain in your own words in what way the sources disagree with each other. If you add to your answer relevant quotes from each source that show the comparison points you have mentioned, then you will get 2 marks.

Now do the same again to make a second comparison and gain a further 2 marks.

6 The Ruhr

What is this chapter about?

France was angry at Germany for the late payment of reparations. In 1923, France and Belgium decided to make Germany pay another way. French troops invaded part of Germany called the Ruhr. The plan was to make Germany work for the French and Belgians directly and so produce wealth that could be taken as reparations. The plan went badly wrong and Germany went into economic meltdown.

By the end of this chapter you should be able to:

- Describe the consequences of the French invasion of the Ruhr.
- Explain why the French invasion of the Ruhr eventually led to hyperinflation.
- Describe the effects of hyperinflation on the German people.

Why were France and Belgium so annoyed that Germany was late paying reparations?

France and Belgium argued that they needed reparation payments to pay for the rebuilding of their countries after the devastation of four years of war. Another reason for wanting reparations was to keep Germany weak. France and Belgium felt safer knowing that Germany could not prepare for a future war.

From Germany's point of view, reparations were a huge, never-ending problem. At first, Germany was told it would have to pay forever, but in 1921 the reparations bill was scaled down. It was still a huge total of £6600 million to be paid in regular instalments well into the 1980s.

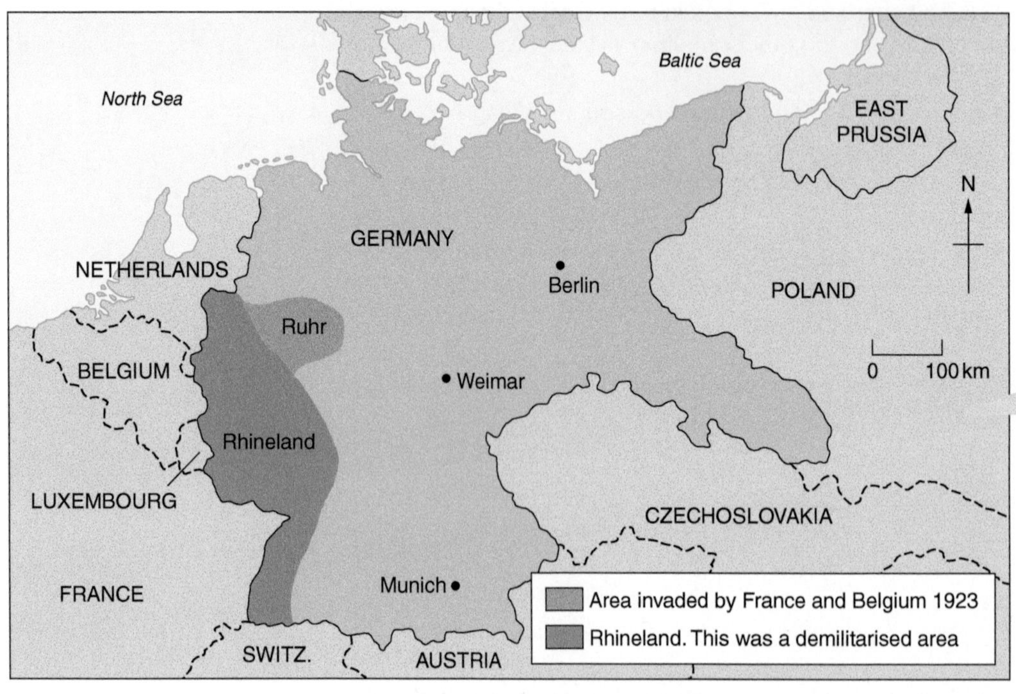

A map showing the Ruhr region of Germany

Given how the Versailles rules applied to the Rhineland, why was the Ruhr under threat from any country that wanted to force Germany to its knees?

Why was the Ruhr invaded?

The **Ruhr** was Germany's industrial heartland that produced most of the country's coal and steel, things that France and Belgium could readily use. It was also easy to invade since it was within the demilitarised Rhineland, meaning that Germany was not allowed to have any soldiers there to protect it. France felt it had good cause to force German repayments since Germany had been late paying for 33 out of the possible 36 months since the reparation arrangements had started.

GLOSSARY

Ruhr a heavily industrialised region of western Germany

Passive resistance resisting by refusing to work for the French

Hyperinflation sudden collapse in the value of German money

Was the French and Belgian invasion of the Ruhr successful?

There were no German soldiers to stop the invasion, but the plan to take German wealth from the Ruhr failed. The German government knew it could not fight back but it did order the workers in the Ruhr to refuse to co-operate with the French and Belgian invaders. This was called **passive resistance**.

How can you tell this is an angry and bitter anti-French cartoon about the invasion of the Ruhr?

Why did the German economy collapse in 1923?

When the workers in the Ruhr went on strike, Germany stopped creating any wealth at all. However, the government continued to pay the workers in the Ruhr simply by printing more money.

In any country there has to be a balance between the amount of paper money being used by the people and the wealth being created by the country. If the wealth being produced falls even slightly then the value of the paper money goes down. It buys less. That is called inflation.

What happened in Germany in 1923 was called **hyperinflation**. There were huge amounts of paper money being printed but no wealth being created. Too much paper money was chasing too few things to buy. Money lost its value completely as prices rocketed to ridiculous and meaningless values. Paper money was even used as toilet paper; it was cheaper and easier to get.

How did hyperinflation affect the German people?

The life savings of many Germans became worthless. They were forced to sell their valuables to buy food. Some workers were paid twice a day. At lunch time, workers roamed the streets hoping to find essentials such as food. If they waited until evening, prices would have gone up again. A German woman trying to feed her family remembered:

On Friday afternoons, workers desperately rushed to the nearest store, where a queue had already formed. When you arrived, sugar cost two million marks but by the time your turn came, it had doubled in price. In the chaos, people pushed prams loaded with money. Life became nightmarish. We were devastated as life savings became worthless. Of course, there were those who were used to having no money but it was hard for those of us who once had money and suddenly had nothing.

Workers who were paid monthly suffered because their income or savings could not keep up with price rises. Instead of using money, people began to barter. You would call it swapping. People would exchange their possessions for things they needed.

Family valuables such as jewellery could be exchanged for enough food for a few days.

People became seriously ill because they could not afford food or heating in their houses. People who rented their houses became homeless because they could not afford rent rises. Many people faced ruin, and depression and mental illnesses swept across Germany like epidemics because of the strain and stress people were under.

Sketch this cartoon accurately. Annotate (arrow and label) at least four features which, when explained, help us to understand the point of the cartoon. Explain your choice of features.

People who depended on being given a set amount of money each week faced homelessness and starvation because they could not afford rent or food. These people included pensioners, disabled people, unemployed people and war widows whose level of income was fixed a few years before. When hyperinflation struck, these people faced ruin.

But not everyone lost out. People who owned property or had big bank loans were not so badly hit. They could pay off their loans easily because the amount of money they were to pay suddenly lost its value.

A German cartoon from 1923. A mother holds up her child and cries out for bread.

Was it fair to blame the government for the hyperinflation crisis?

When Germany lost the war the economy was in a mess and inflation was already a problem long before 1923.

The German public was also unhappy with the new republic. Rightly or wrongly, many people blamed the government for defeat in the war and signing the Treaty of Versailles. The government seemed unable to stop extremist groups such as the Spartacists and the *Freikorps* from bringing violence to city streets.

The government appeared powerless against French troops invading Germany, something that had not happened throughout the whole of the war. When hyperinflation struck it was yet another thing to blame on the new democratic republic.

The Weimar Republic had almost no supporters.

- The working classes hoped for a new Communist government.
- The upper classes wanted a return to something like the Kaiser's strong government before the war.
- In the centre of it all were the middle classes who saw their life savings destroyed almost overnight.

In this atmosphere of discontent, distress and even panic, some political groups thought it would be a good time to get rid of the Weimar Republic and have yet another revolution.

Some of these groups started plotting secretly in Munich, a city in the south of Germany. One of these groups was the Nazis, led by Adolf Hitler.

Activity 1

Summarise this chapter

The following summary reminds you of what this chapter has been about. Words that are important in this chapter have been made into ANAGRAMS. Your task is to sort out the anagrams then write the correct version of this summary into your workbook or work file.

In 1923, soldiers from **ANCEFR** *and* **IUBMELG** *invaded the* **RRUH**, *the* **ILAINDUSTR** *heart of Germany. The reason for the invasion was to make Germany pay* **ATIONSREPAR** *faster. Instead, workers in the* **UHRR** *went on* **KESTRI** *and the* **NEMREG MYNOCEO** *collapsed.* **TNOIINFLPERYHA** *destroyed the value of* **NOMYE.**

Activity 2

If this is the answer what is the question?

Below you will find a list of words or names. You have to make up a question that can only be answered by the word, phrase or number on the list. For example, if the word 'France' was the answer, a question could be 'What was the name of one of the countries that invaded the Ruhr in 1923?'

Here is your list of answers:

- the Ruhr
- reparations
- 1923
- 6600 million
- coal and steel
- strike
- hyperinflation
- barter
- discontent.

Activity 3

- Sketch this picture or a similar one of a distressed person. Around your illustration write as many words as you can find that are connected to the effects of hyperinflation on the German people. Add other words that you think would be relevant to this task.
- Now select a word or phrase to fill in the missing parts shown by the numbers in the summary below. When you have made your choices write out the complete description.

As hyperinflation increased, money became [1]. Workers had to [2] to spend their [3] before prices went up. Germans often [4] for goods as money was worthless. People's savings in the [5] lost their value causing hardship. People couldn't afford [6] and suffered from the cold. Even middle-class Germans couldn't afford [7] so cleanliness suffered. Deaths from [8] were common. Many Germans sold [9] to buy necessities to survive. Finally, those on fixed benefits, for example, unemployed people, suffered badly and many people were reduced to poverty because of [10].

a worthless
b fuel
c rush
d wages
e bartered
f items of value
g soaring prices
h soap
i bank
j hunger

Question practice

National 4

Use Source A and your own research to design a display which shows the following:

- Why many Germans did not like the new system of government that replaced the monarchy.
- What problems Germany faced between 1918 and 1924.

There are a variety of ways you can design this. A few ideas are listed below.

- You could present the information in the form of a leaflet, a spidergram or a storyboard that shows the problems that faced Germany.
- There may also be an opportunity for you to design a slideshow presentation that can be shared with the class or shown on your school's website for revision.
- You could produce your own images and display them on your information poster to make a collage.

Your display should contain the following:

- A description of how the new system of government tried to be fair to everyone.
- An explanation as to why so many Germans were angry with the peace treaty.

SOURCE A

In 1919 the new Constitution promised many things. It promised fairness. It promised a chance for all Germans over 21 to vote. It promised a better voting system based on proportional representation. It promised a voice to every political party, whatever they believed in. In reality, what that meant was that many people were confused. Extremist parties were able to publicise their horrible ideas. The voting system was hard to understand. The peace treaty humiliated Germany. Germans were forced to accept that they were guilty for causing the war all by themselves. And then in the years that followed their life savings were destroyed in the great hyperinflation of 1923.

National 5

The tasks you will have done in Activity 3 are descriptive activities designed to help you answer a 'describe' question. In a 'describe' question you will be asked to describe either what happened or the effects of an event or a development. In this case you had to describe the effects of hyperinflation.

Now, we are going to look at an 'explain' question but from a different angle. Your task here is to WRITE an 'explain' question about the invasion of the Ruhr and the hyperinflation in Germany. Explain questions can start like this: 'Explain the reasons for ...'

You must also write your own mark scheme. That means you must list the points you would expect to see in a good answer. This question is worth 6 marks so you must try to include at least six points in your mark scheme.

When you have completed this task, exchange your work with a partner and answer their question while they answer your question. After ten minutes stop writing, give your work to the person who wrote the mark scheme and he or she will mark your work while you mark their answer.

7 The Munich *Putsch*

What is this chapter about?

In November 1923 the Nazis tried to seize power in the city of Munich in the southern German state of Bavaria. The Nazis were a nationalist group led by Adolf Hitler. Hitler believed that Germans would support the Nazi uprising because they were so unhappy with the Weimar government. The Nazis' attempt to seize power was called the Munich ***Putsch***. A *putsch* is the German word for a takeover of power, usually by force.

By the end of this chapter you should be able to:

- Describe the events of the Munich *Putsch*.
- Explain why the Munich *Putsch* failed.

How does Adolf Hitler fit into the story of Weimar Germany?

When the First World War ended, Hitler was in hospital. He was an ordinary soldier who had been temporarily blinded in a gas attack. Like other loyal soldiers in the German army, Hitler was shocked and angry when he heard that Germany had surrendered. Hitler was 29 years old when the war ended.

At first, Hitler did not want to believe that Germany had lost the war. He agreed with others who said that Germany had been 'stabbed in the back' but he added something else to that idea.

GLOSSARY

Putsch German word for an armed takeover of power

Hitler was born in Austria. At that time there were many Jews in Austria and Hitler was exposed to a lot of anti-Jewish opinions as he grew up. In 1919, Hitler claimed that Germany had lost the war because it had allowed the Jews to have too much power in Germany. He pointed out that Communist ideas had been created by Karl Marx, who was a Jew. He also said that some of the Weimar politicians who had signed the armistice were Jews. However, in 1919 few people listened to Hitler.

Hitler was worried about the Spartacists and other groups that might be plotting to start revolutions in Germany. The army was also worried about these new unknown groups. Soon, Hitler found a job working for the army by spying on one of these groups called the Bavarian German Workers' Party, led by Anton Drexler. At that time it was a small group with no real political ideas apart from disliking the Weimar Republic and wanting to make Germany great again. Hitler quickly gained influence in the party. He learned how to speak to crowds and said what they wanted to hear.

Hitler changed the name of the Bavarian German Workers' Party to the National Socialist German Workers' Party in 1920. It was soon shortened to the nickname Nazi. In 1921 Hitler became leader of the Nazis.

How did Hitler use the hyperinflation crisis to his own benefit?

In September 1923 the German government agreed to negotiate with the French and start paying reparations again. It seemed to be the only way to get out of the economic mess and bring hyperinflation under control. To **nationalists** like Hitler this looked like another surrender and he saw his chance for power.

> **GLOSSARY**
>
> **Nationalists** people who wanted Germany to be stronger and have revenge for the Treaty of Versailles

Hitler had complained about the weakness of the Weimar government for two years. Thousands of young men had joined his organisation hoping for action. If Hitler did not take action now, when discontent with the national government was so high, then his supporters would think he was just another politician who said big things but did nothing.

Hitler decided the time was right to start a revolution to overthrow the national government, but first of all he needed to seize power in Bavaria – and he had competition. Other nationalist groups were also plotting to take power.

Right now, there is huge discontent with the Weimar government.

My supporters are ready for action. If I do nothing, they will drift away from me and all I can do is hope another chance comes along.

If I do nothing, von Kahr will take all the credit if his *putsch* is successful.

It's a no-brainer! **Now** is the time to take action!

Gustav von Kahr was a top politician in Bavaria and he planned to seize control with two powerful friends. One of them was General Otto von Lossow, the head of the army in Bavaria. The other was Colonel von Seisser, who was commander of the Bavarian police. Their main problem was Hitler. The Nazis were attracting unwelcome attention from the Weimar government because of the violent trouble they were causing. Von Kahr and his friends needed to keep Hitler quiet while they plotted their revolution in secret, so they offered him a deal. Von Kahr offered Hitler a place in the new government when they took power. All Hitler had to do was keep the Nazis quiet and stop the street violence. In reality, von Kahr had no intention of giving Hitler anything.

Why was von Ludendorff important?

On the night of 8 November 1923, Hitler heard that von Kahr and his friends intended to hold a big meeting at a beer hall to spark off the uprising – but Hitler had not been invited. Hitler was furious but also realised that the support of the three men was important if the Nazis were to be successful. It was too good an opportunity to miss.

Soon after the meeting started, Hitler and 600 of his supporters, some armed and in uniform, went into the beer hall and lined the sides of the large room. Some witnesses say that Hitler climbed onto a platform and fired shots in the air. He claimed 'The National Revolution has begun!' and that Nazi **Brownshirts** had already taken over important buildings in Munich. However, Hitler knew that the success of his actions depended on what von Kahr, von Seisser and von Lossow did next.

First of all, Hitler ordered the three men to go into a private room away from the crowd. Nobody really knows what happened in the room, but it seems likely that the three men refused to support Hitler. They only changed their minds when General **Erich von Ludendorff**, an old war hero, was brought to the beer hall, apparently to show his support for the Nazis.

Hitler seized his chance and brought von Kahr, von Seisser and von Lossow on to the stage with von Ludendorff, giving the impression that they all now supported the Nazis. With von Ludendorff also supporting the Nazis it looked like success was guaranteed.

GLOSSARY

Brownshirts the Nazi Party's private army

Erich von Ludendorff a military hero of the First World War who reminded many people of the 'good old days' of the Kaiser

This photo shows Hitler (centre in a raincoat) just about the time of the Munich Putsch. Why do you think Hitler was so keen to be associated with von Ludendorff (see next photo)?

Why did the Munich *Putsch* fail?

News reached Hitler that soldiers in the army barracks of Munich were fighting back against the Nazis who had been sent to take control. Hitler now made a disastrous mistake. When he left to see what he could do at the barracks, he failed to make sure that von Kahr and the others were secure.

As soon as Hitler had gone, von Kahr, von Seisser and von Lossow asked von Ludendorff if they could go home to reassure their families that all was well. It was now about 3 a.m. Von Ludendorff foolishly agreed. Once they were free, von Kahr and the others ordered the Bavarian police and army to deal with the Nazis. Later, von Kahr issued a statement saying, 'If the senseless and purposeless attempt at revolt had succeeded, Germany would have been plunged into chaos and Bavaria with it.' Von Kahr and his friends were protecting themselves and leaving Hitler to take all the blame.

When Hitler heard that von Kahr and the others had put all the blame on the Nazis, he was furious but he still believed he could rescue something from the mess. Hitler argued that if the Nazis marched into the centre of Munich they could attract public support. With von Ludendorff at the head of the march the army would never dare fire on them. Hitler had little choice. If they did nothing they would be arrested and the Nazis would lose support.

Early in the morning of 9 November 1923 a procession of Nazi supporters and armed men marched behind Hitler and von Ludendorff. In a narrow street, armed police blocked the Nazis. Shots were fired and 14–16 Nazis and three policemen were killed. Hitler escaped from the scene but was soon captured along with von Ludendorff and others. The *Putsch* was over and the Nazis had failed. Or had they?

Which of the two people is more likely to have wanted this image used, and why?

This picture shows von Ludendorff and Hitler together

Why might you think that this painting was made by a supporter of Hitler? What stage of the *Putsch* does it try to show? Is it factually accurate?

A painting from 1940 showing the 1923 Munich Putsch. *Hitler is in the centre with his arm raised.*

Activity 1

Summarise this chapter

The following summary reminds you of what this chapter has been about. Words that are important in this chapter have been made into ANAGRAMS. Your task is to sort out the anagrams then write the correct version of this summary into your workbook or work file.

In November 1923 the **SNAIZ** tried to seize power in **CHINUM**. Hitler thought this would be a good time because the German people were so **YHAPPNU** with the **RAMWEI** government. The Nazis' attempt to seize power was called the Munich **UTSCHP**. A **SCHPUT** is a German word for an armed takeover of power.

Activity 2

Wordsearch

Make your own larger version of the grid shown here. Draw it large enough so that you can write letters in the boxes.

Use the wordsearch grid to hide five main words, names or ideas linked in some way with the Munich *Putsch*. Complete the grid with random letters to conceal your words and write their definitions below or beside your wordsearch. Do not show where the words are on your grid. Your partner must find them.

When you have completed your wordsearch puzzle, exchange it with your partner's. Read their clues and find the words. As they solve your puzzle, you solve theirs.

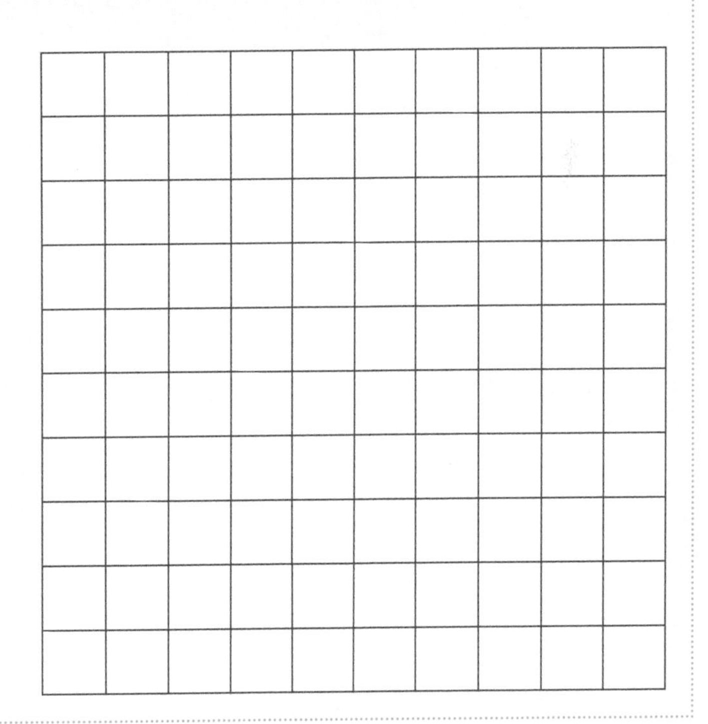

Activity 3

The challenge! How far can you go?

The following questions go up in levels of difficulty in pairs. The first two are easy. The last two are hard. How many will you try to do?

1. Can you suggest another word for *Putsch*?
2. Why did von Kahr want to keep the Nazis quiet for some time?
3. What facts and words used in this chapter show that Hitler was ambitious for power in Germany?
4. How would you summarise the attitudes of von Kahr and his friends towards the Nazis?
5. What evidence could you suggest to support Hitler's decision that late 1923 would be a good time for a revolution?
6. Do you agree with Hitler's actions from the moment he entered the beer hall to the moment he marched towards the soldiers blocking his path the next morning? Give reasons for your answer.

Question practice

National 4

Source A is from Manfred Voorman, from his memoir:

SOURCE A

Most of us in the beer hall were bored and almost asleep as Kahr droned on. Suddenly, Goering and a group of Brownshirts burst into the room and stood, backs to the wall, around the room. Then Hitler came in quickly and before we knew what was happening, he had jumped up on a table, fired his pistol into the air and shouted, 'The National Revolution has begun'. Suddenly we were excited. Things were happening at last.

Describe in your own words the events of the Munich *Putsch*. You should use Source A and your own knowledge.

Success criteria

Write at least two factual points of information, or one developed piece of information, on the events of the Munich *Putsch*.

National 5

Source A was written by a policeman who was present at the Beer Hall *Putsch* in 1923.

SOURCE A

We had heard how Hitler and his Nazis had tried to take over a meeting in the beer hall the night before. We were waiting for them next morning. General von Lossow had escaped from the meeting and warned us what was going to happen. My men forced the Nazis back from our barricade using the batons. Suddenly, one of Hitler's men fired a pistol at my head that missed. Then my men began to fire back. The firing only lasted a few minutes before Hitler's men fled like cowards.

Evaluate the usefulness of Source A as evidence of the reasons for the failure of the Munich *Putsch* in 1923. **(5 marks)**

'Evaluate' means to judge or weigh up the usefulness of a source as evidence for (or against) something. When answering this type of question, it is never enough just to describe what is in a source and you can gain marks by using three different methods.

First, it might be helpful to ask yourself WHO produced the source. Is that relevant in assessing the value of a source? WHEN was the source produced and how might that help in the evaluation of the source? In this case it was from the exact time of the *Putsch*. WHY was the source produced?

You could deal with all those points by writing something like this:

'This source is useful as evidence because it is written by a police eyewitness to some of the events at the Beer Hall Putsch. He is likely to be a reliable witness; however, he was not present inside the Beer Hall because he wrote "We had heard how Hitler ... had tried ..." He is also biased because he calls the Nazis "cowards".'

The second way is to focus on what is useful IN the source, in terms of what the question is asking. In this case you need to find evidence from the source and comment on why the *Putsch* failed. Each piece of evidence and comment will give you 1 mark.

To gain up to 2 marks for this you could write, 'The eyewitness suggests the Putsch failed because they were alerted by General von Lossow who had escaped from the Beer Hall and "warned us what was going to happen". The policeman also reports how his men made barricades to stop the Nazi march and fired back at the Nazis who then "fled like cowards".'

The third way is to write about what makes the source less useful. Think about what could have been included which would have made the source more helpful as evidence in terms of the question. This is worth up to 2 marks. For example, you have already mentioned the policeman only has experience of part of the *Putsch* and is biased. To make the source more effective as evidence of the reasons for failure, it would be helpful to have a Nazi report on what happened, for example, why it took so long for Ludendorff to arrive. That way you are showing off your own knowledge, linking it directly to the question and giving a more balanced evaluation of the source.

8 Who were the Nazis?

What is this chapter about?

Hitler was put on trial for treason after the Munich *Putsch*. At his trial, Hitler used the publicity to make himself nationally famous. Almost overnight Hitler became a household name. When he was sentenced to only a few months in prison it was clear that Hitler had friends in high places. However, the Nazis had to wait almost ten years before they came to power. Throughout most of the 1920s little was heard of the Nazis, but behind the scenes Hitler was planning their triumphant return.

By the end of this chapter you should be able to:

- Explain why Hitler was punished so lightly for his part in the Munich *Putsch*.
- Describe the main Nazi ideas outlined in *Mein Kampf*.

This headline shows that the main news at the time focused on Ludendorff

What does this tell us about the importance of Hitler at the time of the Munich *Putsch* trial?

GLOSSARY

Landsberg the prison where Hitler served his sentence after the *Putsch*

Hitler on trial

Hitler was on trial for treason. If he was found guilty, the sentence should have been death. Instead, Hitler turned the trial into a spectacular success for the Nazis. His statements and speeches inside the trial were reported all over Germany. Hitler explained how he had acted to save Germany from a weak government. Hitler was photographed standing beside von Ludendorff, which made people think that Hitler was an important person. People began to ask who the Nazis were and what they stood for. Look at the two photographs at the top of the next page. Are they really different photos?

The point is that the two photos are identical, but Hitler had the second one cropped so as to make it seem that only he and Ludendorff were important. Why did he do that?

Hitler was, of course, found guilty, but he was given a very short sentence of five years in the fairly comfortable surroundings of **Landsberg** prison. In fact, he was told at his trial he would be able to get parole and be out of prison in nine months. Just a few years before the Munich *Putsch*, Spartacists who had tried to overthrow the government had been executed for the same crime that Hitler was now being gently 'punished' for.

How does Hitler look in the photograph? Think of as many relevant and descriptive words as you can.

At the Munich Putsch trial. General von Ludendorff in the centre with Adolf Hitler on his left. These photos look similar. They were taken at the time of Hitler's trial for treason.

This photo shows Hitler reading a newspaper in prison

Search the internet for 'Hitler in Landsberg prison'. Describe in as much detail as you can the treatment Hitler received in jail. That means his cell, what he was allowed to wear and do, and what items he was allowed to have. Explain why Hitler seems to have been treated so well.

Why was Hitler more or less let off?

It seemed that Hitler had important friends who sympathised with his views and made sure that he was not seriously punished. Remember, it was still only ten years since the start of the First World War and most of the influential people who had been important before the war were still in position in 1924. They hated the new Weimar democracy and also feared Communism. Suddenly, they heard Adolf Hitler speaking their kind of language.

These influential people agreed with Hitler over many points:

- The Treaty of Versailles was disgraceful.
- Communism must be destroyed.
- Democratic politicians had 'stabbed Germany in the back'.
- They wanted Germany to be proud and strong once again.

Those influential, 'behind the scenes' people thought Hitler could be useful to them in the future – so Hitler was let off with a very easy punishment.

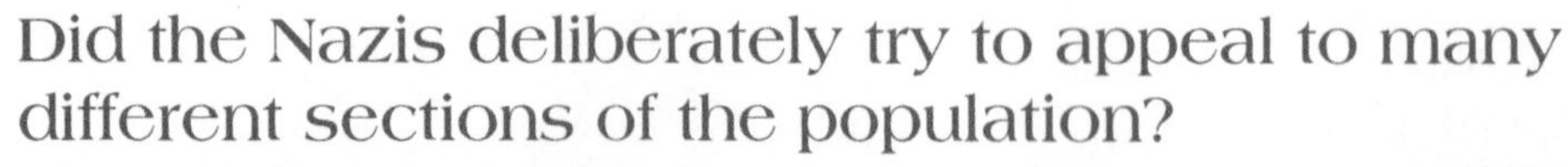

Did the Nazis deliberately try to appeal to many different sections of the population?

Yes, the Nazis tried to be all things to all people. They appeared to be strong and decisive and offer protection against Communism. The Nazi Party's full name is **National Socialist German Workers' Party**. By including the words 'National' and 'German' in its name the Nazis attracted the attention of nationalists. By including 'Socialist' and 'Workers' in the title the Nazis hoped to attract working-class support. The military supported Hitler's ideas of discipline and order. Wealthy businessmen believed that the Nazis would fight the Communists. Powerless people responded to their racist ideas, especially against Jews. Even the Nazi flag was a deliberate creation. Red, black and white were the old colours of the pre-war German Empire. The **swastika** (in its original anti-clockwise form) is an ancient symbol used in old religions in the Middle East and Asia. The Nazis inverted the symbol (making it clockwise) for their purposes, an example of which is shown on the right.

GLOSSARY

National Socialist German Workers' Party the full name of the Nazi Party

Swastika the Nazi badge or logo

Mein Kampf Hitler's autobiography, written while he was in prison

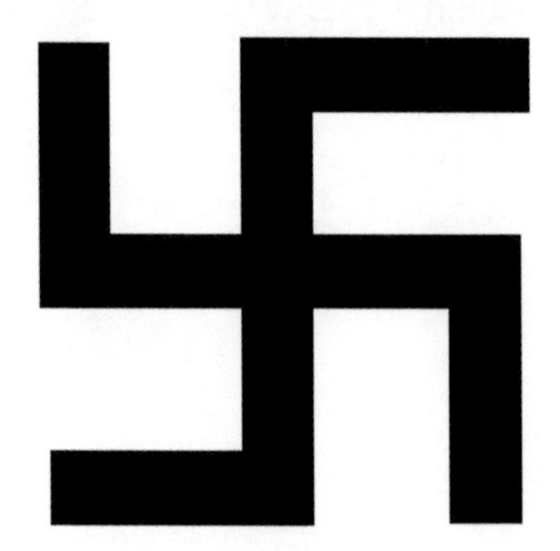

A swastika. The swastika is an ancient religious symbol from the Middle East and Asia.

What did the Nazis stand for?

Hitler used his time in prison to write his autobiography called ***Mein Kampf***. In the book, Hitler outlined his ideas about the future of Germany. He also made clear what the Nazis stood for. He presented Nazi ideas in convincing ways that persuaded people that these simple ideas were the answers to very difficult questions.

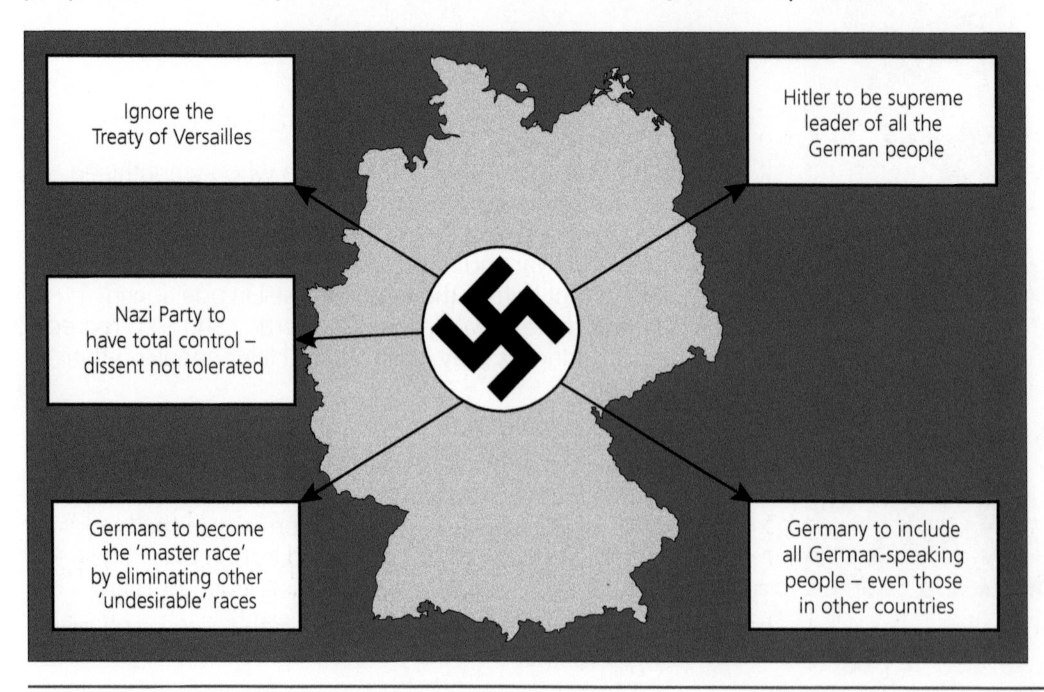

The Nazis' main ideals and objectives

What was the SA?

In 1921 Hitler set up his own private army called the **SA** (Brownshirts). They were mostly young men, some of whom had been members of the *Freikorps*. The SA attracted men who wanted action and that often meant violence. The SA was intended to protect Nazi meetings, but SA members often started the violence and attacked the meetings of political opponents, especially Communists. Germans who were afraid of Communists were relieved when the Nazis took action against them.

> **GLOSSARY**
> **SA** *Sturmabteilung*, the Nazi private army, also known as the Brownshirts

How did Hitler plan to destroy the Weimar Republic?

While he was in prison, Hitler made an important decision about future tactics. The failure of the Munich *Putsch* in 1923 convinced Hitler that the only sure way of getting greater power was by legal means. He is reported as saying, '... we shall have to hold our noses and enter the *Reichstag*'. In other words, Hitler would campaign for power legally and destroy the system from within. He is also credited with saying that outvoting the opposition would take longer than outshooting them but the result would be the same: power.

Another way of describing Hitler's new plans is to say he wanted the Nazis to act like a Trojan horse.

> In what sense can Hitler's plan to win seats in the *Reichstag* be compared to the Greek plan to use a wooden horse?

The story behind the Trojan horse

You have probably heard of the word Trojan in the sense of a virus that gets into a computer's hard drive and then destroys the files. The reason for the term is because the virus operates like the Trojan horse of thousands of years ago. At that time the city of Troy (in present-day Turkey) was at war with Greece. The Greek army tried for many months to capture Troy but failed. One day they made a big show of packing up and sailing away. The Greeks left a gift on the beach to show respect to the Trojans (the people of Troy). The gift was a huge wooden horse. The Trojans were delighted. They had won. They pulled the big wooden horse into their city, celebrated victory and went to sleep. That night a trap door opened and Greeks hidden inside the horse climbed out. They opened the city gates and let in the Greek army that had crept back under cover of darkness. The city of Troy was destroyed. The Trojan horse had helped to destroy Troy by getting inside and destroying it from within!

A model of the Trojan horse

How important were the Nazis in the mid-1920s?

So far, you have read about Hitler and the Munich *Putsch*, how Hitler gained national publicity at his trial, how he received a light punishment for trying to overthrow the government and how he reorganised the Nazi Party on his release from prison. This all sounds very much as if the Nazis were poised to take power at that point. The truth is that the Nazis were a very unimportant party in the mid-1920s.

Most people had lost interest in the Nazis after Hitler was sent to prison. It is only because we know what happened in the following few years that we mistakenly think the Nazis must have been more important than they were at this moment in time. Hindsight – using our full knowledge of what occurred – only makes us seem smart because we know what happened next. People at the time could not possibly have known with any certainty what might happen.

By 1928 the Nazi Party had still not broken through into national politics in a big way. Out of more than 600 representatives from all the various parties in the *Reichstag* there were only 12 Nazis. Less than three per cent of German voters voted for them. In comparison, the Social Democrats held 153 seats in the *Reichstag* and even the Communists had almost 50 seats.

Activity 1

Summarise this chapter

The following summary reminds you of what this chapter has been about. Words that are important in this chapter have been made into ANAGRAMS. Your task is to sort out the anagrams then write the correct version of this summary into your workbook or work file.

Hitler was found guilty and sentenced to **EVIF EARYS**. He was imprisoned in **NDSBERGLA** where he wrote **INME PAMFK**. His autobiography made clear the main ideas of the **INZA** Party. While in prison Hitler decided his best chance of gaining power was to be **TEDELEC** legally and then destroy German **CRACYMEDO** from **WINITH**.

Activity 2

Look carefully at the earlier diagram showing the swastika and the main ideas of the Nazis. Copy out the statements and after each one, write clearly whether you agree with the statement or not and give a reason for your decision.

- The Nazis wanted to keep Europe peaceful and stable.
- Hitler was to be the sole leader of a Nazi Germany.
- Hitler wanted to help all Germans and give them a safe and secure home.
- If the Nazis came to power, Germany would become a dictatorship.
- Nazi ideas would destabilise Europe and make it a dangerous place.
- Nazis were intolerant of people different from themselves.
- Germany's neighbours were right to be worried if the Nazis came to power.
- The Weimar Republic would be destroyed if the Nazis came to power.

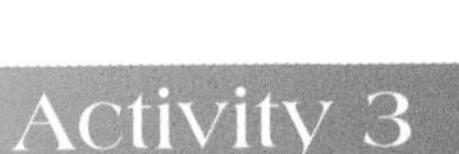

Activity 3

Work in pairs. In this activity make up at least five questions that you would use to test someone's understanding of the Nazis and their ideas.

To make up the questions, first work out what you want to ask. You must also have a clear idea of what answer you want for your question. Avoid questions that are vague and have no focus such as 'What do you think about the Nazis?' A good question would be 'What did the Nazis think about the Treaty of Versailles?'

Avoid questions that ask 'Who was …' or 'When was …' Also don't ask questions that have one-word answers – they are not allowed!

Your questions should be mature, well presented and test real understanding. The purpose is to help learning, not to catch people out with really tricky questions.

When you have both completed five questions, try them out on each other. Can your partner answer your question? And can you answer your partner's question in return? The ones to remember are the questions you could not answer. They provide a guide to what you are less sure about and are therefore a guide to revision.

Repeat this exercise either now or at a later date – and try it out on different topics.

Question practice

National 4

Source A was written by a recent historian about the results of the Munich *Putsch*.

SOURCE A

The failure of the Munich Putsch in 1923 convinced Hitler that the only sure way of getting more power was by legal means. While he was in prison Hitler made an important decision about future tactics. He is reported as saying, 'we shall have to hold our noses and enter the Reichstag'. In other words, Hitler would campaign for power legally and destroy the Weimar Republic from within.

Describe the effects of the failure of the Munich *Putsch*. You should use Source A and your own knowledge.

Success criteria

Write at least two pieces of information explaining the results of the Munich *Putsch*.

National 5

Describe the aims of the Nazi Party in the mid-1920s. (4 marks)

This type of question is worth 4 marks.

To be successful you should try to write four separate, accurate points of information that are relevant to the question asked. For example, *'One aim of the Nazi party in the mid-1920s was to unite all German-speaking peoples.'* [1 mark]

If you can't remember four different points to write about, you could write more detail about the points you can remember.

For example, to develop the idea about uniting all German-speaking peoples you could write, *'Of course, German-speaking people lived in countries outside Germany, so the Nazis' aim to unite all Germans might mean taking over other countries.'*

9 The golden age of Weimar

What is this chapter about?

Between 1924 and 1929 things got much better for the Weimar Republic, so much so that this time was called the 'golden age of Weimar'. Most of the improvement was due to the work of Gustav Stresemann, the new German Chancellor. He was helped by an American politician called Charles Dawes who had arranged large loans to help Germany to recover from hyperinflation. Germany seemed to be recovering and was about to enter a golden age.

By the end of this chapter you should be able to:

- Describe how the work of Charles Dawes and Gustav Stresemann helped Germany to recover.
- Explain why there was very little public support for the Nazis in the middle and late 1920s.

Did hyperinflation just go away?

The German economy did not simply heal itself. The recovery was the result of the work of two men: one German, the other an American.

The American was Charles Dawes. Economists across Europe and in the USA realised that if the German economy was left in ruins then the whole economy of Europe was unstable. The problem of reparations also had to be sorted out. Trade had slumped and a wrecked Germany could not even begin paying any reparations.

Charles Dawes' plan arranged for the USA to lend Germany a great deal of money, to be used to get the country back on its feet. In August 1924, the Dawes Plan arranged for:

Was Dawes the man who created the **golden age** of Weimar?

- French and Belgian occupying troops to leave the Ruhr
- reparation payments to begin again at one billion marks in the first year, increasing to two and a half billion marks each year after five years
- the ***Reichsbank*** to be reorganised and a new paper currency introduced.

Charles Gates Dawes (1865–1951), photographed circa 1924. He was Republican Vice-President of the USA under Calvin Coolidge.

Was the Dawes Plan a success?

Yes – at first. The Dawes Plan provided short-term economic benefits to the German economy and made reparations easier to pay. The new paper money gave German people confidence and businesses and employment started to recover. As the German economy grew, international confidence in Germany increased and so more foreign loans were available. More people had jobs and had money in their pockets to spend. It seemed as if the bad old days were over.

GLOSSARY

Golden age a time when things went very well; the Weimar Republic had a golden age between 1924 and 1929

Reichsbank the main German bank

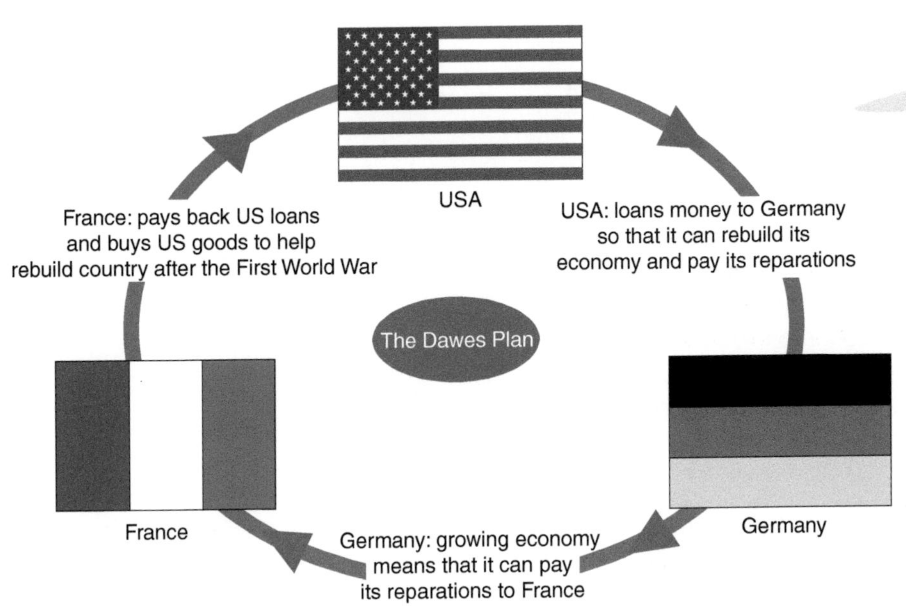

A diagram showing the way the Dawes Plan helped Germany to recover after hyperinflation

Any break in the cycle would cause economic problems, but a break in which part of the circle would cause *most* problems? Explain your choice with reasons.

The start of Weimar's golden age

Why was Gustav Stresemann so important to Germany?

The other man closely linked to Germany's recovery in the 1920s is Chancellor Gustav Stresemann. Stresemann is still thought of as the man who created the golden age of Weimar by doing three main things:

- He sorted out the economy.
- He made Germany internationally respectable.
- He gave the German people pride and confidence in the future.

GLOSSARY

Rentenmarks new German currency to replace the worthless old money

How did Stresemann sort out the economy?

Stresemann brought hyperinflation under control. He ordered that all the old bank notes be collected and burned. He issued new notes, called **Rentenmarks**. Stresemann also got a political boost when German industry recovered once the French and Belgians agreed to leave the Ruhr. Most of these things would not have happened without the Dawes Plan. Nevertheless, Stresemann helped to restore confidence in the German currency. Once people had confidence in their money, then they would save and that would allow banks to use the money to invest in new German businesses. Finally, in 1929 Stresemann reached another agreement with the USA to reduce reparation payments further as part of the Young Plan.

A German cartoon

Make up your own caption to summarise what this cartoon shows.

How did Stresemann make Germany internationally respectable?

Stresemann took on two jobs in the Weimar government. Not only was he chancellor, he also became foreign minister, which meant he was in charge of Germany's relationships with other countries.

> **GLOSSARY**
>
> **Locarno Treaty** a 1925 treaty in which Germany tried to make better relations with its neighbours

Stresemann knew that Germany's neighbours such as France were deeply suspicious of Germany and were afraid that if the country recovered, it might start causing trouble again. To reassure Germany's neighbours that they had nothing to fear, Stresemann signed a new treaty at Locarno in 1925.

The **Locarno Treaty** was a big move towards peace in Europe because, until that time, Germany had repeatedly said that it did not accept the diktat Treaty of Versailles and wanted to change it. That made France very distrustful of Germany. In the Locarno Treaty, Germany accepted the Treaty of Versailles as it affected western Europe, in exchange for a promise from France and Belgium never again to invade Germany. Stresemann knew that by saying Germany accepted the treaty, the rest of Europe would relax and Germany would no longer be the 'outsider' in Europe.

> Why is Stresemann still thought of as a German hero? Stresemann died in 1929, ten years before the start of the Second World War. Do you think Stresemann could have prevented the war if he had lived?

In 1926 Stresemann made Germany even more internationally respectable when the country became a full member of the League of Nations. It looked as though Germany had apologised for the First World War, had accepted its punishment and now wanted to be on friendly terms with its European neighbours.

How did Stresemann restore pride and confidence in the German people?

People liked the idea that the USA trusted Germany with loans. These loans helped to create jobs, which in turn paid wages to thousands of Germans. Between 1924 and 1929 Germany was increasingly prosperous. People were happy to support the new democratic republic as long as it 'delivered' in terms of improving wages and living standards, and making sure there was enough food to eat.

The voting figures for the Nazis at this time showed that people had simply lost interest. For example, the Nazis had only 14 representatives in the *Reichstag* in 1924 and that fell to 12 by 1928. During the golden age of Weimar fewer than three per cent of German voters voted for the Nazi Party.

So what went wrong? Why did the Weimar Republic end in 1933, only four years after it seemed to be going so well? The new and improving German economy was heavily dependent on the USA. How would Germany cope if anything happened to the USA?

A propaganda poster symbolising the treaty between France and Germany by Gustav Stresemann to evacuate the Rhineland

Activity 1

Summarise this chapter

The following summary reminds you of what this chapter has been about. Words that are important in this chapter have been made into ANAGRAMS. Your task is to sort out the anagrams then write the correct version of this summary into your workbook or work file.

The years between 1924 and 1929 are called the **EHT NEDLOG EGA FO AIREMW.** *Two men helped Germany to recover –* **LESCAHR SEDAW** *and* **VATSUG NAMNSTREES.** *The real reason for Germany's recovery was the arrival of* **SLOAN** *from* **ICAMERA.**

Activity 2

If this is the answer what is the question?

Below you will find a list of words or names. You have to make up a question that can only be answered by the words on the list. For example, if the word 'Dawes' was the answer, a question could be 'What was the name of the plan that arranged US loans for Germany in 1924?'

Here is your list of answers:

- Charles Dawes
- *Rentenmark*
- Gustav Stresemann
- golden years
- USA
- Locarno
- confidence
- 14
- 12.

Activity 3

Design a revision mobile

Your mobile should illustrate the changing fortunes of the Weimar Republic between 1918 and 1928. You can choose to work on your own or as part of a group no bigger than four. If you work in a group, you must also design and use a creativity log in which you record exactly what each person in the group contributed to the final mobile.

In practical terms, the best structure is usually two criss-crossing wire coat-hangers.

Success criteria

- Your mobile must have at least four strands.
- Each strand should be about a main theme in the story of the Weimar Republic such as 'Versailles' or 'Golden years'.
- Each strand should have several mobile items attached.
- Each strand must have two text items, each containing significant names or words.
- Each strand must have at least one large, double-sided illustration linked to an event or a person.
- Each strand must have a three-dimensional feature that represents a major event.
- Your mobile should hang easily.
- Your mobile must be readable from a distance.
- Your mobile must be attractive, colourful and relevant to the project task.

Question practice

National 4

Use the historical information in this chapter and anything else you can discover to design an information poster. This information poster should show the following:

- What problems Germany faced before 1924.
- What Stresemann and Dawes did to make life in Germany better.

There are a variety of ways you can design this. A few ideas are listed below.

- You may wish to divide your information poster into 'before' and 'after' the work of Stresemann and Dawes.
- Or, you could present the information in the form of a leaflet, a spidergram or a storyboard that details the story of Germany before 1924.
- There may also be an opportunity for you to design a slideshow presentation that can be shared with the class or shown on your school's website for revision.
- You could produce your own images and display them on your information poster to make a collage.

It is important to remember that you will only be assessed on your historical understanding and not on the artistic qualities of your information poster. However, it should be presented in a clear and neat manner to allow your audience to fully understand your main arguments.

National 5

How important was the work of Gustav Stresemann in creating a golden age for Weimar Germany in the mid-1920s? (9 marks)

This type of question is worth 9 marks. 'How important' questions are very similar to 'How successful' and 'To what extent' questions.

To be successful with this type of question, you need to decide how important a particular factor – in this case, Gustav Stresemann – was in explaining why Weimar Germany experienced a golden age in the mid-1920s. This means you should mention positive things about the work of Stresemann, but then balance your answer by considering other events that helped Germany which had nothing to do with Stresemann directly.

A straightforward way to get maximum marks here is to start by writing that the work of Stresemann was PARTLY the reason for Weimar Germany entering a golden age in the mid-1920s. You should aim to give up to five pieces of relevant, accurate information to support the idea that Stresemann was important.

Here are some points you could mention:

- Hyperinflation under control.
- Old bank notes to be collected and burned.
- New notes, called *Rentenmarks*.
- Restoring confidence in the German currency.
- Work as foreign minister reassuring Germany's neighbours that they had nothing to fear.
- Treaty of Locarno 1925.
- Germany becoming a full member of the League of Nations.

You should then balance your answer by using the following clues to give other reasons for German recovery such as:

- The Dawes Plan arranged for the USA to lend Germany a great deal of money to get the country back on its feet.
- Loans helped to create jobs, which in turn paid wages to thousands of Germans.
- French and Belgian occupying troops left the Ruhr.

To get 9 marks you must:

- have an introduction [1 mark]
- have five pieces of relevant, accurate/factual information [5 marks]
- organise your knowledge into 'for' and 'against' the idea in the question [1 mark]
- make a judgement on the question [1 mark]
- support your judgement by summarising the reasons you have given [1 mark].

SECTION 2

The Nazi rise to power 1929–1933

10 The path to chancellor

What is this chapter about?

At the beginning of 1929 all seemed to be going well for the Weimar Republic. Why then did the republic end in 1933, only four years later? Part of the answer lies with two big problems that hit Germany in 1929. The first problem was the collapse of the US economy. The USA's crisis soon became a worldwide catastrophe. The second problem was the sudden death of Gustav Stresemann, the man who had guided Germany out of its previous economic crisis in 1924. When the German economy collapsed again in 1929, the public listened to the one man who appeared to promise them safety and security: Adolf Hitler.

By the end of this chapter you should be able to:

- Describe the economic and political problems facing Germany by 1932.
- Explain why Hitler was asked to be chancellor in January 1933.

Why did problems in the US economy affect Germany?

Throughout the 1920s, the US economy had been booming, but in October 1929, the value of the US economy collapsed almost overnight. This became known as the **Wall Street Crash**, named after the financial heart of the US banking system in Wall Street, New York. It was the start of the **Great Depression**. As the US economy faced crisis, American banks wanted to get back all the money from loans they had made to other countries, including Germany.

GLOSSARY

Wall Street Crash the Great Depression started with the collapse of the US stock market based in Wall Street, New York

Great Depression a time of worldwide, high unemployment following an economic collapse in the USA starting in 1929

Why was the death of Stresemann a serious problem for the Weimar Republic?

Stresemann had got Germany out of a mess during 1923–24, so when he died in October 1929, shortly before the financial crisis hit, the Weimar Republic lost its most able leader. Stresemann had also successfully improved Germany's international reputation and had eased the reparations bill that Germany had to pay. He had been a force for European peace and had made strong personal friendships with other European politicians.

What words would you use to describe how the people are reacting? What words would describe their thoughts? What words would describe the thoughts and feelings of Germans in the coming months?

The Wall Street Crash as illustrated in an Italian magazine in 1929

If Stresemann had lived and remained in the German government, it might have been possible to control Hitler and limit the rise of the Nazis. You will find out in the next chapter that many Weimar leaders thought they could control Hitler, but in reality, they were too weak.

How did the US financial crisis help the Nazis?

In 1928, the Nazis only had 12 seats in the *Reichstag*. However, by 1930 their seats had increased to 108. Clearly something must have happened to make people vote for the Nazi Party in such large numbers. The 'something' that allowed the Nazis to increase their support was the economic crisis that swamped Germany after 1929.

Germans feared the return of hyperinflation. The economic crisis of 1923 has been described as being like a cut that never healed. The Germans had got used to prosperity, jobs, wages and good times based on loans from the USA. Earlier in 1929 a new plan, the Young Plan, had seemed to guarantee Germany further US help. Now, later that year, the economic crisis hitting Germany was much worse than the situation in 1923, as there was no chance of any outside help. Germany had to pay back its loans much faster than expected and as a result, shops, banks and factories collapsed and began to close.

As times got worse for Germany, Hitler saw a chance to gain support. He claimed that the Nazis had the answer to all of Germany's problems and that the Weimar government was just making things worse.

Make a sketch copy or trace this. Replace the German slogan with your own appropriate slogan. Choose three people in the poster and make speech bubbles for them. In each bubble place a reason why they might vote for Hitler.

An election poster for the Nazi Party from 1932

In Germany, the government's policy of cutting government spending only made the problems facing ordinary Germans much worse. Unemployment began to rocket. By 1932, six million Germans were unemployed and people were willing to listen to any political group which promised work and food – such as the Nazis.

Many historians claim that without the economic crisis, the German people would not have voted for the Nazi Pary. One historian, A.J.P. Taylor, wrote that 'It was the Great Depression that put the wind in Hitler's sails.' In other words, if the Great Depression had not happened, then the Nazis would not have won so much support.

How did the financial crisis that hit Germany weaken its democracy?

In the spring of 1930, President Hindenburg appointed Heinrich Brüning as **chancellor**. For most of the next two years Brüning and his advisers ruled Germany without even getting the agreement of a majority of politicians in the *Reichstag*. This was called ruling by decree.

The constitution of the Weimar Republic was meant to guarantee that the German government was fair and honest. However, Article 48 of the **Weimar constitution** allowed the president to take total control of the government in an emergency and let the chancellor rule by decree. Article 48 was meant to help, but it severely wounded democracy in Germany and helped Hitler come to power.

GLOSSARY

Chancellor the leader of the German government

Weimar constitution the rules set up to run the new Weimar Republic

By 1932, the government was changing almost every few months. The democratic parties could not agree on how to deal with Germany's problems. The economy was in ruins, unemployment was rising and the politicians seemed to be ignoring the democratic ideas on which Weimar Germany was based. As a result of those feelings of discontent, many Germans lost faith in democracy and looked for any political party that offered answers to their problems.

Did Hitler come to power just because of the Great Depression?

Another reason for the growth of the Nazi Party is that important people supported the Nazis with money and publicity because they thought the Nazis could be useful to them. One such person was a politician called Alfred Hugenberg, the leader of the German People's Party, known in Germany as the DNVP.

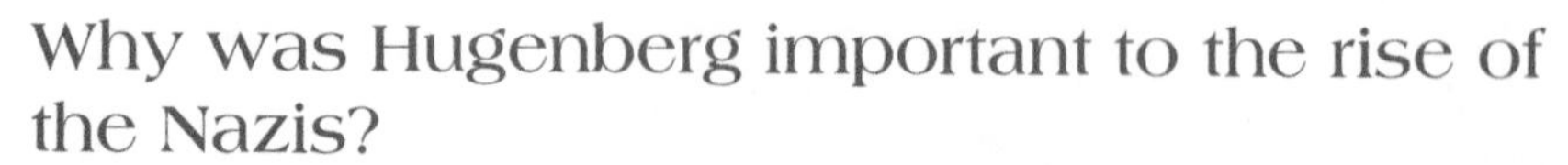

Why was Hugenberg important to the rise of the Nazis?

Hugenberg saw the Nazis as a strong group that could stop the Communists – by violence if necessary. Hugenberg also thought he could use Hitler to get publicity for his own nationalist political beliefs. As a result, Hugenberg poured money into a huge publicity campaign to promote the Nazis.

Hugenberg owned most of Germany's new cinema industry and hundreds of local newspapers. Every day, Hugenberg could arrange for Hitler to be front-page news all across Germany. In the cinema, Hitler and the Nazis could be on every newsreel shown. In the early 1930s, cinemas were the only places people could see the news and people went two or three times a week. In short, Hugenberg gave the Nazis national publicity.

Explain the meaning of this cartoon in terms of Hitler's rise to power.

The media publicity given to the Nazis by Hugenberg made the Nazis known across all of Germany. As a result, the Nazis were also given huge amounts of money by wealthy businessmen who were impressed by the images of Nazis in the cinema and the reporting of their ideas in newspapers and on radio.

Hitler often claimed that '... millions stand behind me'. One meaning of this was that millions of people supported the Nazis. But opponents of the Nazis claimed what Hitler really meant was that millions of Deutschmarks from big business gave the Nazis financial power to fight national elections.

A cartoon called 'Mr Hitler's backers' showing Hugenberg helping Hitler to mount a horse

How did politicians help Hitler become chancellor?

There were three politicians within Weimar Germany who really opened the door for Hitler's rise to power.

The first was **President Hindenburg**. Hindenburg was a national hero but by 1932 he was an old man not always clear in his thinking. Hindenburg did not even like Hitler and believed that he was a threat to democracy.

The second was **Franz von Papen**, who became chancellor for a short time and hoped to use Hitler for his own political advantage.

The third politician involved in Hitler's rise to power was **General von Schleicher**. He was an ambitious army general who wanted to become chancellor and needed Hitler on his side to get public support.

In 1932 Franz von Papen replaced Brüning as chancellor and immediately asked the president to rule Germany under emergency laws. When the Nazis won 230 seats in the *Reichstag* out of a total of 608, von Papen realised that allying with the Nazis would conveniently bring with it the support of Nazi voters – or so he thought. Von Papen was so confident he could control Hitler that he said, 'In six months we'll have pushed Hitler so far into a corner he will be squealing.' Von Papen was wrong. Hitler had no intention of being controlled.

Von Papen had political enemies, one of whom was General Kurt von Schleicher. Von Schleicher was no supporter of democracy and made many secret arrangements with politicians in order to increase his own power. Von Schleicher also hoped to control Hitler. When von Papen could not get Hitler's clear support von Schleicher forced Papen to resign. Von Schleicher, in turn, also misjudged Hitler. When von Schleicher was made chancellor he tried to limit the activities of the Nazi Party. In retaliation, Hitler joined with von Papen to defeat von Schleicher.

Why was Hitler made chancellor?

By the end of 1932 Hindenburg had no choice: both von Papen and von Schleicher had failed to build a government. Meanwhile, the Nazis were manipulating the *Reichstag* and making Germany ungovernable. The Nazis were the biggest political party in the *Reichstag*. It was easy for Hitler to order his Nazis to walk out of the *Reichstag* at a moment's notice and force yet another election. When Hitler was offered the job of **vice-chancellor** he refused. He had no intention of being linked to a crumbling system without the power to change it.

Hindenburg did not like Hitler and knew the Nazis would destroy democracy, but he had no options left. It looked as if Hitler and his Nazis were the only people with answers. Hindenburg was persuaded to appoint Hitler as chancellor of the Weimar Republic on 30 January 1933.

Who are the three main characters? Why are the two that are walking looking unhappy? Explain what the position of the sitting person's hands represents. What event is this cartoon commenting on? Does this cartoon do a good job in explaining fully Hitler's rise to power?

A cartoon from a British magazine called Punch in January 1933

GLOSSARY

Vice-chancellor the second in command to the chancellor

The interrelations of German politicians during the early 1930s

Activity 1

Summarise this chapter

The following summary reminds you of what this chapter has been about. Words that are important in this chapter have been made into ANAGRAMS. Your task is to sort out the anagrams then write the correct version of this summary into your workbook or work file.

The **LLAW EETSTR CHASR** *sparked off a world economic crisis. In Germany* **MANNSTRESE** *died and Germany was left leaderless. President* **BURGHINDEN** *did not like Hitler and tried at first to give the job of* **LORLCHANCE** *to* **NOV ENPAP** *and then to* **NOV HCRESCHLIE.** *Both those people failed in the job and Hindenburg was forced to appoint* **LITHER** *as chancellor in January 1933.*

Activity 2

The challenge! How far can you go?

The following questions go up in levels of difficulty in pairs. The first two are easy. The last two are hard. How many will you try to do?

1. Who or what were the main problems facing Germany in 1929 and 1930?
2. How did Alfred Hugenberg help Hitler and the Nazis?
3. Why did the use of ruling by decree weaken the basic ideas of democracy in the Weimar Republic?
4. Using what you now know, how would you explain why Hitler became chancellor?
5. Just by looking at the votes given to the Nazis between 1928 and 1930, what conclusions can you make about the fears and worries of many German voters?
6. Design a diagram to show the relationship between Hindenburg, von Papen, von Schleicher and Hitler. Your diagram should show how they felt about each other and also how they may have needed each other.

Activity 3

Teach a lesson

In groups of three or four, your target is to teach a short lesson to the rest of your class which is linked to the theme of Hitler's rise to power.

You must deal with the following core points:

- How did the crises of 1929 help to revive Hitler and the Nazis?
- In what ways was democracy undermined before Hitler became chancellor?
- Why did Weimar politicians think that Hitler could be useful to them?
- Why was Hitler made chancellor in January 1933?

As in any lesson, there are really important things for you, as the teacher, to decide on and aim for:

- What do you want your students to be able to do and know at the end of your lesson?
- How will you assess the success of your lesson – in other words, what will you expect to see or hear your students doing to prove your lesson has been successful?

Your lesson should be presented in an organised, interesting, mature and informative way. Your main resource for information is this textbook, but you must also research, find, beg or borrow other resources to make your lesson come alive. Think of the times you have been bored just listening to someone talk. Your lesson must be different! Planning is vital, and everyone in your group must participate. It would be helpful to assign tasks such as a gopher to go get, a timekeeper to watch how your time is being used, a facilitator to keep things running smoothly in your group (tact and diplomacy needed here!) and a recorder to note ideas before you all forget.

Negotiate the length of your lesson with your teacher. About five minutes would be appropriate. It must have visual material; PowerPoint is just one of the possibilities.

Question practice

National 4

Source A is from Michael Wolowitz, a television presenter.

SOURCE A

Hitler would never have achieved power if there had not been such high unemployment. Yes, publicity helped him but it was the Great Depression that made people think that Hitler might be the answer to their problems.

Source B is from G. Baker, a historian writing about Hitler's rise to power.

SOURCE B

Hitler was put in power by the plotting of others. Hugenberg built up Hitler by showing him in his cinemas and newspapers. Weimar politicians created Hitler. Without these selfish politicians, Hitler would never have come to power.

Compare the views in Sources A and B about Hitler's rise to power. Describe in detail their similarities and/or differences. You can also briefly compare the overall attitude of the sources.

Success criteria

Use the two sources in order to show two simple points of comparison, or one developed point of similarity or difference.

- An example of a simple comparison is: 'Source A says ... and Source B says ...'.
- An example of a developed comparison is: 'Sources A and B disagree about the reasons for Hitler's rise to power. Source A says ... and Source B says ...'.

National 5

Explain why Hitler was popular with many Germans. (6 marks)

This 'explain' question is worth 6 marks. To be successful you should try to give six different reasons based on recall that must be relevant and accurate.

The main thing to remember in this question is to provide reasons WHY Hitler was popular with many Germans. A useful tip to remember is to use the word 'because'. After 'because' you cannot help but write a reason for something, so in this case you could write, '*One reason why Hitler was popular with many Germans was because he promised to rip up the Treaty of Versailles.*' [1 mark]

You can always get an additional mark by developing a reason you give. That means you give extra detail to support the point you are making. For example, '*Many Germans saw the Treaty of Versailles as humiliating and the cause of many of the problems that followed. Hitler, therefore, became popular by promising to restore German pride and destroy the treaty.*' [1 extra mark]

11 From chancellor to dictator

What is this chapter about?

Between January 1933 and August 1934, Hitler made himself dictator of Germany. There were very clear steps in Hitler's climb to dictatorship. The *Reichstag* fire allowed Hitler to take extra powers for himself and the Enabling Act moved Germany ever closer to dictatorship. After the Night of the Long Knives, Hitler gained the support of the army, and when Hindenburg died, Hitler finally destroyed Weimar democracy and created a Nazi dictatorship.

By the end of this chapter you should be able to:

- Explain why Germany could be described as a dictatorship by the end of 1934 but not at the beginning of 1933.
- Describe the steps by which Hitler became more powerful between January 1933 and August 1934.

How did Hitler set about destroying the Weimar Republic?

Hitler had always intended to destroy the democratic Weimar Republic; now he set about doing it.

Although Hitler was chancellor, the Nazis still did not dominate the *Reichstag* or the government of Germany. The Nazis still needed support from some smaller parties. Hitler knew that one of his first problems would be the Communists. They were attracting many voters and challenged the Nazis for seats in the *Reichstag*.

ALL THE NEWS THAT'S FIT TO PRINT

Jersey Times

Latest news

VOL. CLVIX . . No. 70,631 — TUESDAY, JANUARY 31, 1933 — TWO CENTS

HITLER MADE CHANCELLOR OF GERMANY

BUT COALITION CABINET LIMITS POWER;

CENTRISTS HOLD BALANCE IN REICHSTAG

GROUP FORMED BY PAPEN

Lorem ipsum dolor sit amet, consectetuer adipiscing elit. Aenean commodo ligula eget dolor. Aenean massa. Cum sociis natoque penatibus et magnis dis parturient montes, nascetur ridiculus mus. Donec quam felis, ultricies nec, pellentesque eu, pretium quis, sem. Nulla consequat massa quis enim. Donec pede justo, fringilla vel, aliquet nec, vulputate eget, arcu. In enim justo, rhoncus ut, imperdiet a, venenatis vitae, justo. Nullam dictum felis eu pede mollis pretium. Integer tincidunt. Cras dapibus. Vivamus elementum semper nisi. Aenean vulputate eleifend tellus. Aenean leo ligula, porttitor eu, consequat vitae, eleifend ac, enim.

Headline in a US newspaper of 31 January 1933

How does the headline about Hitler becoming chancellor make clear that Hitler was still very far from being a dictator?

Hitler's first aim was to increase the number of Nazis in the *Reichstag* so new elections were set to be held in early March 1933. However, with the election only a few days away, the *Reichstag* suddenly burst into flames.

Who started the Reichstag *fire*?

When the police arrived at the fire they discovered a 24-year-old Dutchman, Marius van der Lubbe, beside the burning building with matches and fire-lighters in his pockets. He was arrested and when found guilty, he was beheaded.

Ever since then, historians have argued about van der Lubbe's guilt. It seems likely that he did start some fires, probably encouraged to do so by the Nazis. However, all his fires went out. The main fire started well away from where van der Lubbe had been. So who started the main fire and why?

How would this photograph published in German papers be useful to Hitler?

Why was the *Reichstag* fire helpful to Hitler?

When Hitler heard about the fire he immediately claimed that the fire was a Communist plot and that Communists were planning to start a revolution. Hitler said, 'There will be no mercy now. Every Communist official will be shot where he is found. Everybody supporting the Communists must be arrested.'

Within hours of the fire, Hitler arrested around 4000 Communists. Whether there was any real Communist plot hardly mattered. It was enough for Hitler to claim that Germany was under threat from terrorist attack.

Now, all Hitler had to do was get President Hindenburg to use Article 48 of the Weimar constitution. Almost immediately, Hindenburg agreed and the *Reichstag* Fire law was passed. Officially it was called a 'Decree for the Protection of the People and the State', but it did nothing to protect the German people from the real threat: Hitler and the Nazis. The new law destroyed many of the **Fundamental Laws** created by the Weimar constitution. Newspapers could be **censored** and even private letters and phone calls could be checked. Newspapers belonging to the political opponents of the Nazis were closed down.

The Reichstag *building in flames*

As the election got closer, the German people were bombarded with anti-Communist propaganda while the Communists themselves had their offices smashed and printing presses – used to print posters and newspapers – destroyed.

The result of the election was never in doubt. Hitler had used the *Reichstag* fire to scare the German people into believing that only Hitler could protect them. Many Germans now believed the Nazi propaganda about a Communist plot to start a revolution and as a result, the Nazis won 288 seats in the election, more than they had ever gained before.

Hitler was now in a very strong position.

GLOSSARY

Fundamental Laws the basic laws of the Weimar Republic that guaranteed Germans their civil rights

Censored information that is cut, restricted or withheld

Enabling Act gave Hitler the power to act as a dictator for four years

Why did Hitler need the Enabling Act?

Hitler and the Nazi Party had won the March 1933 election with five million votes more than before, but the Nazis *still* did not have a majority in the *Reichstag*. The Nazis had to rely on 52 votes from their coalition partner, the German National People's Party, in order to get Nazi policies made in to law. From Hitler's point of view, that had to change.

When the new Nazi-led government met after the March election, plans were made for an **Enabling Act** that would give the Nazis law-making powers for four years. The Enabling Act allowed Hitler to make new laws without asking the *Reichstag*. Hitler would no longer have to rely on other political parties in the *Reichstag*.

The Enabling Act was a temporary law, meant to allow the chancellor time to save Germany from a political emergency. Once the emergency was over, Hitler was expected to give power back to the elected *Reichstag*. In reality, Hitler had no intention of handing power back.

How did Hitler use the Enabling Act to create a total dictatorship?

The Enabling Act of 23 March 1933 allowed Hitler to rule like a dictator. Within three months of the act, Hitler banned all parties except the Nazi Party. By the middle of July 1933, the Nazi Party was the only political party allowed in Germany. Hitler banned trade unions because he thought they were organisations that might oppose the Nazis. He ordered **concentration camps** to be built to imprison anyone who he thought might oppose him. By the end of 1933, over 150,000 political prisoners were in concentration camps.

Hitler had created a dictatorship by legal means. However, he still worried about the German army and the SA.

GLOSSARY

Concentration camps large prisons for anyone who opposed the Nazis

SS Hitler's personal bodyguards that grew to the size of an army

Night of the Long Knives On 30 June 1934, Hitler arranged for the murder of anyone he believed was a threat to him

How did Hitler kill two birds with one stone?

The SA was led by Ernst Röhm, an old friend of Hitler. Röhm was ambitious. He wanted to break up the regular army and put all Germany's soldiers under SA control. Hitler was worried. He feared the army officers might be provoked into leading a revolution against the Nazis. Put simply, the SA's leaders were becoming a problem to Hitler – they had to go.

What was the 'Night of the Long Knives'?

Hitler came up with a solution for his problem.

On the night of 30 June 1934 Hitler commanded the **SS** to kill many of his enemies. Those 'enemies' were simply anyone who had annoyed or opposed him in the past such as von Schleicher and von Kahr from the time of the Beer Hall *Putsch* 11 years earlier. The dead also included his old friend and leader of the SA, Ernst Röhm.

The mass murder of the SA leadership was called the **Night of the Long Knives**.

Why was the Night of the Long Knives useful to Hitler?

First of all, the destruction of the SA pleased the regular army. Hitler now felt more secure. Secondly, the Night of the Long Knives was an important step on the road to total dictatorship. Hitler claimed that his victims had been planning to overthrow him. Just after the murders Hitler was sure enough of himself to say quite openly that he gave the order '... to shoot the ringleaders in this treason'. It is possible that up to 400 people were murdered under Hitler's orders.

What do you think the cartoonist is trying to say about Hitler's actions? Do an internet search for other cartoons about the Night of the Long Knives. Are there any other images that you think are better than the cartoon shown here? Why is your choice better?

'Will the audience kindly keep their seats.' A cartoon by Sidney Strube, published in the Daily Express, 3 July 1934.

What does '*Der Führer*' mean?

President Hindenburg died on 2 August 1934. Hindenburg's death marked the end of the democratic Weimar Republic. Just before Hindenburg died, Hitler's government had passed a law combining the roles of president and chancellor. In the Weimar Republic the roles of president and chancellor were separate and each balanced the other. Now, in Hitler's Germany, the posts were combined and Hitler transformed into *Der Führer* – the supreme leader and dictator of Germany.

The combination of the two roles had been forbidden by the Weimar constitution, so to make the change more respectable a **plebiscite** was held on 19 August 1934. The 'yes' vote reached 90 per cent. Did that mean Hitler had huge support? Or did it mean that people realised that Hitler was already all-powerful and to do anything to oppose him would be dangerous?

GLOSSARY

Plebiscite a referendum or vote by the people about one question

Oath a very serious promise

How did Hitler ensure the army's loyalty?

Within hours of Hindenburg's death Hitler arranged for every individual member of the armed forces to swear this **oath** of loyalty to Hitler:

I swear by God this sacred oath that to the Leader of the German people, Adolf Hitler, supreme commander of the armed forces, I shall render unconditional obedience and that as a brave soldier I shall at all times be prepared to give my life for this oath.

Members of the army had previously sworn loyalty to 'the People and the Fatherland'. Now they swore an oath of personal loyalty to Hitler.

Between January 1933 and August 1934, Hitler had carried out his promise to destroy the Weimar Republic from within. He had created a dictatorship and now it looked as if nothing could stand in his way.

Hitler addressing the crowds at the Nazi Party convention in Nuremberg, Germany, 10 September 1935.

Do you think this photograph is an effective way to end this chapter?

Activity 1

Summarise this chapter

The following summary reminds you of what this chapter has been about. Words that are important in this chapter have been made into ANAGRAMS. Your task is to sort out the anagrams then write the correct version of this summary into your workbook or work file.

In January 1933 Hitler became **CARCONHELL** *of Germany. Within 18 months Hitler had made himself* **RERFUH**. *The* **GSTAEICHR RIFE** *gave Hitler an reason to take more power. The* **INGBLENA TCA** *gave Hitler the power of a dictator for four years. In June 1934, the* **THGIN FO ETH ONGL SNEVIK** *removed Hitler's enemies and it also* **LEASPED** *the* **MYAR**. *Finally, Hitler made himself* **REFUHR** *when* **BGURHINNED** *died and the army swore an* **THOA** *of* **YALTYOL**.

Activity 2

Design a staircase diagram. It could be as simple as a series of steps up a diagonal line.

At the bottom write 'Chancellor' and the date when Hitler took on that job.

At the very top write '*Führer*' and the date when Hitler took on that role.

In between, plan how many steps you will need to show the main stages in Hitler's rise to total power. On each step or stage write clearly the date and the event which took Hitler ever closer to being dictator of Germany. Clue: you must have at least five steps.

Activity 3

Work in pairs or a group of four. In this activity make up at least ten questions that you would use to test someone's understanding of Hitler's rise to power.

To make up the questions, first work out what you want to ask. You must also have a clear idea of what answer you want for your question. This is to avoid questions that are vague and have no focus such as 'What do you think about Hitler?' A good question would be 'Why was the death of Hindenburg an important step in Hitler's rise to power?'

Avoid asking questions that ask 'Who was …' or 'When was …' Also don't ask questions that have one-word answers – they are not allowed.

Your questions should be mature, well presented and test real understanding. The purpose is to help learning, not to catch people out with really tricky questions.

When you have completed ten questions, try them out on each other. The ones to remember are the questions you could not answer. They provide a guide to what you are less sure about and therefore are a guide to revision.

Repeat this exercise either now or at a later date – and try it out on different topics.

Question practice

National 4

Source A is what Hitler was reported to have said when told about the *Reichstag* fire.

SOURCE A

There will be no mercy now. Anyone who stands in our way will be cut down. Every Communist official will be shot where he is found. Everybody supporting the Communists must be arrested.

Give reasons to explain why Hitler thought the *Reichstag* fire could be useful to him. You should use Source A and your own knowledge.

Success criteria

Write at least two pieces of information explaining how the *Reichstag* fire was helpful to Hitler.

National 5

This is a 'describe' question. In this type of question you will be asked to describe either what happened or the effects of an event or development.

Describe the results of the *Reichstag* fire. (4 marks)

This type of question is worth 4 marks.

To be successful you should try to write four separate, accurate points of information that are relevant to the question asked. For example, '*One result of the Reichstag fire was to give Hitler an excuse to demand more power to deal with the emergency.*' [1 mark]

If you can't remember four different points to write about, you could write more detail about the points you can remember.

For example, to develop the point about getting more power, you could write, '*Hitler claimed there was a Communist plot and the Reichstag Fire Law was passed to let him deal with the emergency.*' [1 extra mark]

Top tip: answer the question! The question does not ask you to describe the fire. It is about what happened *afterwards*. Always answer the question that you are asked, *not* the one you would like to be asked.

Helpful clues: when planning your answer, you could look at the immediate, short-term results such as the attack on Communists and the results of the March election or you could look more widely at how the fire helped Hitler's further rise to power in 1934. In fact, you could even write about the short- and long-term effects in your answer, but remember to make clear the connection between the fire and the result you are describing.

SECTION 3

Nazi control of Germany

12 Nazi Germany: fear and force?

What is this chapter about?

The Nazis were in power in Germany between 1933 and the end of the Second World War in 1945. Between 1933 and 1939, Hitler created a totalitarian dictatorship. This meant that the Nazis had total power over everything that happened in Germany. In the previous chapter you found out why many Germans were happy to go along with this. This chapter is about what happened to those people who were not prepared to accept Nazi rule. It also raises a question: did most Germans accept Nazi control because they supported it, or because they were too scared to do anything about it?

By the end of this chapter you should be able to:

- Describe how the Nazis used fear and intimidation to keep control.
- Explain why people were afraid to oppose the Nazis.

Why were so many Germans afraid to speak out against the Nazis?

Many Germans were intimidated – or frightened – into accepting Nazi control. Underneath the rallies and the **propaganda**, Hitler deliberately created a climate of fear in Germany. Any organisation or individual who spoke out against the Nazis inside Germany was silenced. All political parties, except the Nazi Party, were banned. By the end of 1933, 150,000 political prisoners were in concentration camps.

The most feared areas of Nazi control were the ***Gestapo*** and the concentration camps, run by the SS.

The *Gestapo* was started in 1933 as the secret police force of the Nazis. They were responsible for rounding up Communists, Jews and any others who were considered to be a threat to the Nazi state. The *Gestapo* was also feared because of its use of torture to gain confessions from suspects.

GLOSSARY

Propaganda influencing people with a simple, one-sided argument

Gestapo the Nazis' secret state police force

Gestapo members dressed in ordinary clothes so the German people didn't know when they were being spied on. Nor did they know which of their friends or neighbours would report what they said. There were never as many *Gestapo* members as people thought there were. There did not need to be. It was enough for people to believe that they were being spied on to make them afraid and to suspect every stranger of being part of the *Gestapo*.

How does this painting try to show how Hitler controlled Nazi Germany?

A 1933 painting by Mexican artist Diego Rivera

Some reports suggest there were up to 45,000 people in the *Gestapo*, but its real power lay in the number of informers and special agents it used. Up to 160,000 people were employed by the *Gestapo* to inform on friends and neighbours or anything they suspected was anti-Nazi.

Why did people inform on their friends and neighbours? Occasionally, when a person was arrested, the *Gestapo* put pressure on their families to inform on other people. At other times people informed on their friends for a small bribe or to protect their own families. Sometimes it was because people wanted revenge for personal arguments and jealousies.

Nobody was sure where the *Gestapo* was operating, but stories swept through towns about friends and relatives who mysteriously vanished when the *Gestapo* arrived at their door.

The result was that people kept their mouths shut and their opinions to themselves. They did not want to be taken away to concentration camps.

GLOSSARY

Dachau the first Nazi concentration camp

The concentration camps

In the early years of Nazi Germany, concentration camps were places where the Nazis sent political opponents such as socialists, Communists and trade unionists. Conditions were at first just like an uncomfortable prison, but soon they became places of torture and murder as the camps filled up with anyone the Nazis did not like.

Nazi Germany's first concentration camp was built at **Dachau**, a village a few miles from Munich, but soon many other camps were built all across Germany.

The camps were filled with people described by the Nazis as 'undesirables' and the prisoners' clothes were marked with colour-coded badges so as to identify the reason for their imprisonment:

- red for political prisoners
- green for criminals
- black for those considered to be anti-social
- pink for homosexuals.

It was only later, during the Second World War, that the concentration camps became places of mass murder of Jews during the Holocaust.

A modern-day memorial to prisoners of the Dachau concentration camp

The concentration camps were an important part of the fear that the Nazis used to keep control over the German population. Most Germans never saw a concentration camp, but it was enough to know that these places existed and that people could vanish from their homes in the middle of the night and would never be seen again. The concentration camps were places to be feared and were yet another form of intimidation used to ensure the German people did not cause trouble for the Nazis.

The *Gestapo* and concentration camps were the most feared parts of Hitler's **totalitarian state**. Behind the scenes, Hitler destroyed the civil rights and individual freedoms that people had enjoyed under the Weimar Republic. Once the people started to miss those freedoms, it was too late.

A group of political prisoners held at the Dachau concentration camp by the Nazis for their opposition to the German regime

What is a police state?

Hitler created a totalitarian state. That means a government (also known as a state) that has total control over everything in the country. Nazi Germany was also a police state. That meant the Nazi government controlled the lawmakers, the courts and the police. In other words, the Nazis had the power to make laws, to enforce the laws and to decide who was guilty of breaking the laws.

GLOSSARY

Totalitarian state a state that controls everything and does not allow opposition

This photograph shows Germans being stopped, searched and perhaps being taken away in the waiting truck by police and the Gestapo

How does this photo show control of the population by fear? Would you be happy to live in a state that did this sort of thing regularly and randomly? What if the state said it was necessary for your security? Try to explain your ideas as fully as you can.

The ordinary German people could say and do nothing against the state. All they could do was shout their approval of the Nazis at rallies or keep quiet if they disagreed. At least that was the theory. In reality, some people and organisations did oppose the Nazis – but not many.

The police state used fear and punishment to enforce obedience. For most people it was just too dangerous to do anything to show you were against the Nazis.

How is living in Britain different from living in Nazi Germany?

Britain is a democratic country. In a democratic country the police should not take sides in political arguments. In Nazi Germany the police were ordered to help the Nazis and persecute any opposition.

In a democratic society, adults elect a government and there are opposition parties who can criticise the government. In Nazi Germany there was no freedom of speech and no political opposition.

In a democratic society, citizens cannot be arrested unless they have broken the law. They must be charged with a crime and be allowed to prepare a defence. In Nazi Germany people were kept in prison with no idea of why they were there or when they would be released. German citizens had no right to a defence. There was no attempt to be fair. Basic justice was denied to the German population.

In a democratic society, judges are meant to make unbiased decisions based solely on evidence. In Nazi Germany judges were told they always had to support Nazi ideas and punish anyone the Nazis disapproved of.

It seemed as if there was nothing anyone inside Germany could do to oppose the increasing power of the Nazis, yet some people did try.

Activity 1

Analysing photographs

Are people who protest just making life difficult? Would you ever protest strongly? Why? Or why not? Which of these two protests would you support?

Activity 2

Summarise this chapter

The following summary reminds you of what this chapter has been about. Words that are important in this chapter have been made into ANAGRAMS. Your task is to sort out the anagrams then write the correct version of this summary into your workbook or work file.

The Nazis used **ARFE CRAND FOE** to control Germans who **SEDOPPO** Nazi rule. The **GEAPOST** spied on the population and anyone who expressed any anti-Nazi ideas was put in one of the new **NATION AMPSCOC CENTR**. Nazi Germany was a **ICE POLE TATS** which means … (complete yourself).

Activity 3

If this is the answer what is the question?

Below you will find a list of words or names. You have to make up a question that can only be answered by the word on the list. For example, if the word 'fear' was the answer, a question could be 'What word would describe one way the Nazis controlled the German population?'

Here is your list of answers:

- intimidated
- Gestapo
- concentration camps
- freedom of speech
- police state
- judges
- justice
- totalitarian state
- colour-coded badges.

Activity 4

The Nazis had a saying that summed up what a totalitarian state was:

Nothing outside the State,

Everything within the State,

Nothing against the State.

There are two parts to this activity.

1. Rewrite, using different words, this three-line statement so that it contains the same ideas but is presented in different language. The Nazi saying is memorable and short and makes its point clearly. Your version must have the same advantages.
2. Design a graphic presentation of the ideas you have just written about. Your graphic can be in the style of a graphic novel, a single cartoon, a flowchart or any other format that puts across ideas in a visual style. Somewhere in your presentation you must include the rewritten statement you did in part 1.

Question practice

National 4

Source A is from historian Amelia Mitchell about how the Nazis kept control by using force and fear.

SOURCE A

Nobody spoke openly. If anyone did, they had to say good things about the Nazis or they might be overheard. Then they could be arrested and sent to one of the new prison camps. Nobody seemed to come back from these places.

Describe how the Nazis used fear to control the German population. You should use Source A and your own knowledge.

Success criteria

Write at least two pieces of information describing how fear was used by the Nazis to keep control.

National 5

Source A is adapted from the memories of a concentration camp prisoner in 1936.

SOURCE A

When we arrived at the camp, we were all extremely tired and very worried. Initially, the camp commander seemed quite reasonable. Once we had all lined up, he explained that we had nothing to fear so long as we did as we were told. He ordered us to leave our valuables on the ground in front of us. We were not happy about this and my friend complained. Immediately, the commander took out his pistol and shot my friend dead on the spot. He then calmly reminded us of the need to follow orders, or else there would be 'consequences'.

How fully does Source A describe the Nazi use of fear and intimidation as a way of controlling Germany between 1933 and 1939? (6 marks)

This question is worth 6 marks. To answer this type of question you could start by writing, 'The source PARTLY describes fear and intimidation as used by the Nazis to control Germany.'

That counts as a judgement in terms of the question which asks 'How fully ...'

You then need to find three pieces of relevant information from the source that describe the use of fear and intimidation. You could mention that the author of the source was in a concentration camp, and that he witnessed a man being shot dead for speaking. You might also mention the feeling of threat the source author must have felt on being forced to part with his valuables. That will gain you 3 marks.

To balance your answer you then need to write up to four extra pieces of information from your own knowledge that are relevant to the question but which have not been mentioned so far in the source. For example, you could mention the Gestapo and the use of informants.

13 Opposition to the Nazis

What is this chapter about?

By the end of 1933, 150,000 political prisoners were in concentration camps. All other political parties were banned. Any organisation or person who spoke out or did anything against the Nazis inside Germany was punished. The Nazis wanted no opposition to their rule over Germany. Recently, historians have calculated that roughly 77,000 German citizens were killed by the Nazis for resisting. Why did so many people risk their lives opposing the Nazis? On the other hand, why did a far greater number of Germans not resist the Nazis? Many of the answers link back to what you have learned in previous chapters. Many Germans liked their new life under the Nazis. Only a few were prepared to risk everything and take a stand against the Nazis.

By the end of this chapter you should be able to:

- Describe some of the groups that did oppose the Nazis.
- Explain why opposition to the Nazis was so difficult.

Why was there so little opposition to the Nazis within Germany?

The Nazis were overwhelmingly popular with the German people

Nazism gave many Germans what they wanted: money, food and jobs. As a result, they were prepared to accept the Nazi dictatorship as it spread over all aspects of life in Germany in the 1930s. The word for just accepting something even if you don't like it is **acquiescence**. Germans who did not actively support the Nazis simply acquiesced. They did not oppose. They just 'went with the flow'.

GLOSSARY

Acquiescence accepting something

Censorship controlling news and information so that Germans knew only what the Nazis wanted them to know

Resistance being against something

Hitler had destroyed the hated Treaty of Versailles and made Germany strong again. German troops reoccupied the Rhineland area of Germany in 1936 and took over Austria in 1938. Both of these things had been forbidden by the Treaty of Versailles.

It is also true that many people did not know the bad things that were going on. **Censorship** stopped people from receiving reliable information. Newspapers openly criticising the Nazis were banned, their offices closed down, reporters arrested and printing machinery smashed. The extreme policies of the Nazis were kept secret. Meanwhile, Nazi propaganda told them the Nazi state was a huge success.

Finally, the Nazis had been democratically elected and that caused many Germans to think that the Nazis had the legal right to do what they wanted.

There was no united or effective political opposition

Almost as soon as Hitler came to power, Communists and Social Democrats were banned. Their leaders were forced to leave the country or were put in prison and party members were afraid to meet each other to organise any **resistance** to the Nazis.

The Communist Party and the Social Democratic Party were also unable to unify in the fight against Hitler. Their dislike of each other went back to 1919 when the Social Democratic leader, Ebert, had ordered the destruction of the Spartacists. As a result, the two parties failed to unite against Hitler in elections, and by 1933, it was too late to stop him.

Spies and informers spread insecurity

The Nazis built up a network of informers. Every group, village or club within Nazi Germany had its informers who would report anything that was against the Nazis, even just an anti-Nazi joke or complaint. It was soon obvious to everyone that even the slightest indication of discontent would make it difficult to find a job or gain promotion within the Nazi state – so people kept their mouths shut.

Any opposition groups that did exist were small scale because any contact with strangers risked discovery by informants and spies. Even small children were encouraged by their teachers to betray their parents if any anti-Nazi comments were made at home.

Almost every person in Germany knew about people who had been taken away to concentration camps, so it was no surprise that they did not speak out for fear of what might happen to them. A common saying at the time was 'Dear Lord God, keep me quiet, so that I don't end up in Dachau.'

What do you think this image means in the context of what people did and did not feel safe talking about in Nazi Germany?

Sssssh! Speak only through a flower

Who did oppose the Nazis?

Most resistance to the Nazis consisted of small and usually isolated groups. The most famous anti-Nazi youth movement was known as the White Rose (*Weisse Rose*) movement formed by students at Munich University. Its leaders were siblings Sophie and Hans Scholl. They published anti-Nazi leaflets, but the group were caught fairly quickly, put on trial and executed. Today, the members of the White Rose are honoured in Germany among its greatest heroes, since they opposed Hitler's regime in the face of almost certain death. Sophie Scholl was only 22 years old when she was beheaded by the Nazis.

Members of the White Rose: Hans Scholl, Sophie Scholl and Christoph Probst, who were all executed

Would you risk everything, including your life, to protest against something you knew to be very wrong? If you have been really honest with your answer, how do you now feel about yourself?

Another group, the Red Orchestra, consisted of anti-Nazis and Communists who began to help their Jewish friends as early as 1933. There were also organised gangs of teenagers who opposed Nazi control.

Who were the Edelweiss Pirates, the Meuten and the Swing Kids?

The Edelweiss Pirates were groups of young Germans who refused to co-operate with the Nazi state. They gave themselves names such as the 'Roving Dudes' and the 'Navajos'.

The Pirates were working-class boys and girls approximately aged between 14 and 18 years old who did not want to take part in the activities of the Hitler Youth. Instead, they formed gangs who knew and trusted each other because they lived or worked in the same area. In Cologne, the Navajos sheltered army deserters and concentration camp escapees. The Pirates specialised in attacking Hitler Youth groups wherever they found them – hiking and camping in the countryside or Hitler Youth patrols in the towns.

The *Meuten* (which means packs) were gangs with wider anti-Nazi political aims. In the city of Leipzig, the *Gestapo* estimated there were 1500 *Meuten* members between 1937 and 1939. Since the *Meuten* gangs aimed to destroy Nazi control, they faced much harsher Nazi reprisal than some of the other youth groups.

There were also the Swing Kids. They were mostly male teenagers who loved listening and dancing to 'un-German' swing music, blues or jazz. Nazis claimed that such music was 'black music' and as such would pollute Aryan youth and undermine Nazi teaching about the inferiority of black people. The Swing Kids tried to wear the latest American- or English-style clothes and accepted Jews into their groups. Swing clubs sprang up in most big cities despite persecution by the Nazis.

Finally, there was the resistance network within the German army. These groups hatched conspiracies against Hitler in 1938 and again in 1939, but army officers found it hard to think of resistance because they had sworn a personal oath of loyalty to him in 1934.

Another group that was torn between supporting Nazism, acquiescing or opposing was the Church in Germany. That is covered in the next chapter.

Do you think this is an effective poster? Try to judge it from the point of view of the 1930s, and especially in light of Nazi racist ideas. Do you think the Swing Kids were just self-interested or were they a genuine anti-Nazi opposition group?

This Nazi poster is attacking American jazz music, popular with Swing Kids

Activity 1

Summarise this chapter

The following summary reminds you of what this chapter has been about. Words that are important in this chapter have been made into ANAGRAMS. Your task is to sort out the anagrams then write the correct version of this summary into your workbook or work file.

Most people did not **SEOPPO** the Nazis either because they were too afraid or because the Nazis improved their lives. The Nazis did have some opposition from political groups such as **COM TINS SUM** and **COAL IS DOCS TAMER** but they were banned and soon could not exist in Germany. Teenage gangs such as the **METUNE** and the **DIE WE LESS RATS PIE** carried out small-scale attacks on Hitler Youth groups. Meanwhile, the **WINGS DISK** were not so much against Nazis as against being told what to dance to and how to dress.

Activity 2

If this is the answer what is the question?

Below you will find a list of words or names. You have to make up a question that can only be answered by the word on the list. For example, if 'Swing Kids' was the answer, a question could be 'Which youth group showed their opposition to the Nazis by dancing and dressing fashionably?'

Here is your list of answers:

- Edelweiss Pirates
- opposition
- acquiesce
- *Meuten*
- the oath of loyalty
- Scholl
- White Rose
- informants
- Roving Dudes.

Activity 3

You are a member of the White Rose group working with Hans and Sophie Scholl. You know you are risking your life, but you feel you must do something against the Nazis. Your chosen way of protest is to design small, short leaflets that try to make the German people wake up to the reality of Nazi control.

The only way you have of getting your message to the public is to throw leaflets from tall buildings or from railway carriages. Your leaflets must be eye-catching and make people want to read them. The content must contain information that you want people to know and think about. People cannot be seen reading the leaflets, so the content must be quickly and easily understood. The best way is to keep text information short, have a big heading and perhaps include some sort of graphic. Most importantly, your leaflet must make people want to do something to oppose the Nazis, and stop acquiescing. Create a leaflet, knowing your life is now at risk.

Question practice

National 4

Source A is about the lack of opposition to the Nazis. It is by a German woman living in Berlin.

SOURCE A

There was just no opposition. Everyone seemed to support the Nazis. Those who did not like the Nazis kept their mouths shut ... or maybe they were dead.

Source B is by Louis Jordan, a swing musician.

SOURCE B

Every week kids risked punishment just for coming to our club and dancing to our music. They went wild. It was one way to show that not everyone was a good Nazi.

Compare the views in Source A and Source B about opposition to the Nazis.

Success criteria

- Examine two sources in order to show two simple points of comparison or one developed point of similarity or difference.
- An example of a simple comparison is: 'Source A says ... and Source B says ...'.
- An example of a developed comparison is: 'Sources D and E disagree about opposition to the Nazis. Source E says ... and Source F says ...'.

National 5

Explain the reasons why it was so difficult to oppose the Nazi government after 1933. (6 marks)

This 'explain' question is worth 6 marks. To be successful you should try to give six different reasons based on recall that must be relevant and accurate.

The main thing to remember in this question is to provide reasons WHY it was so difficult to oppose the Nazi government after 1933. A useful tip to remember is to use the word 'because'. After 'because' you cannot help but write a reason for something, so in this case you could write, '*One reason it was so difficult to oppose the Nazi government after 1933 was the difficulty of getting accurate information about what was really happening in Germany.*' [1 mark]

You can always get an additional mark by developing a reason you give. That means you give extra detail to support the point you are making. For example, '*Censorship and the banning of newspapers by the Nazis meant that news and information was strictly controlled.*' [1 extra mark]

14 The churches in Nazi Germany

What is this chapter about?

Hitler tried to control the Christian churches in Germany. Some people believe Hitler wanted to replace Christianity with Nazism. While the Nazis tried to reach agreement with the Catholic Church, they aimed to create a new 'Nazi-approved' Protestant Church in Germany. Some priests, ministers and pastors accepted Nazi interference. A few may even have agreed with some Nazi ideas. But others within the churches actively resisted the Nazis.

By the end of this chapter you should be able to:

- Describe how the Nazis tried to control Christian churches in Germany.
- Explain why some church members seemed to accept the Nazis at first but later on began to strongly oppose the Nazis.

How did the Nazis feel about the German churches?

The Nazis wanted complete control over German life and the Church stood in their way. Some Nazis felt that the Church should be destroyed, but Germany was a very Christian country. The Nazis would have faced huge difficulties if they had tried to destroy the Christian churches. Nearly all Germans were Christians with roughly 33 per cent Catholics and 66 per cent Protestants. In 1933, the Protestant Church had more members than any other organisation in Germany, including the Nazi Party.

The Nazis did make some attempt to create a new **pagan** religion to replace Christianity. It was called the German Faith Movement and involved a pagan-style worship of nature and the sun. The Nazis even created new pagan ceremonies for marriage, baptism and burials, but they never caught on with the wider population.

GLOSSARY

Pagan not believing in the God of the Bible, Torah or Koran

How did the Church feel about the Nazis at first?

Some church leaders thought the Nazis could be useful to them. Communists did not believe in God and believed organised religion was just a way of keeping the population quiet and obedient. Catholics especially hated Communists so they were pleased when the Nazis attacked Communists.

On the other hand, many church people spoke out against Nazi abuse of human rights.

What is this cartoon about? Try to decide why the cartoonist chose to draw the cartoon in this way.

A cartoon published in the Daily Mirror *in 1941*

The Protestant Church

Church members argued over how much they should co-operate with the Nazis. This was made all the more difficult as there was no single Protestant Church. In fact, there were 28 different Protestant groups in 1933. As a result, there was no co-ordinated Protestant opposition to the Nazis. To gain control over the German Protestant Church, the Nazis created a new **German Christian Church** led by Ludwig Müller. In April 1933 he was given the title of 'Reich Bishop'.

The German Christian Church played an important role in the persecution of the German Protestant Church. German Christians adopted Nazi-style uniforms and marches.

> **GLOSSARY**
>
> **German Christian Church** a new, Nazi-approved Christian church led by Ludwig Müller, the 'Reich Bishop'
>
> **German Confessional Church** a new Christian church against the Nazis led by Martin Niemöller

The Nazis were also concerned about the role of Christian youth organisations and the influence they had over the youth of Germany. Since these organisations were rivals to the Hitler Youth, the Nazis wanted to abolish them. On 17 December 1933 by the order of the Reich Bishop, the entire Protestant Youth Movement with more than 700,000 members was placed under the leadership of the Hitler Youth.

Protestant opposition

The attempt to control the Protestant Church failed. Many bishops and pastors (church ministers) refused to yield to pressure. Opposition in the Protestant Church against the Reich Bishop caused Müller to fade in importance, but control of the Church passed more directly to the Nazi Ministry for Ecclesiastical Affairs.

The majority of the ministers who attacked Hitler and the Nazis in their speeches and writings were silenced by being put into concentration camps or by being prohibited to speak or write.

Many German Protestants were unhappy about the way Hitler had hijacked their church and in 1934, 200 pastors who believed political parties should not control the Church established the **German Confessional Church**.

Martin Niemöller and the Confessional Church

Among the leaders of the Confessional Church was Pastor Martin Niemöller. Niemöller spoke out against Hitler and the Nazi abuses of human rights. It was difficult for the Nazis to silence Niemöller as he had been a First World War U-boat captain and war hero.

Niemöller tried to make people aware of what was happening and stop them just 'burying their head in the sand'. His poem, 'First they came for the Jews' is still quoted today when people speak up for others who are being persecuted.

First they came for the communists
and I did not speak out –
because I was not a communist.

Then they came for the trade unionists
and I did not speak out –
because I was not a trade unionist.

Then they came for the Jews
and I did not speak out –
because I was not a Jew.

Then they came for me
and there was no one left
to speak out for me.

By 1937 Pastor Niemöller had been arrested and put in a concentration camp. As Niemöller had been a war hero, Hitler gave orders for him to be left alive. Niemöller survived the war and continued to speak out against human rights abuses long after the war ended.

What is this book referring to? What does it mean? Explain why the publishers chose the title shown here for this book.

HITLER came for NIEMÖLLER The Nazi War Against Religion

This book was written in 1942 by Leo Stein about Pastor Niemöller

Other religious opponents of the Nazis were not so fortunate. Many of them were held in concentration camps and several were executed. One such person was Dietrich Bonhoeffer, who was one of the leading Protestant ministers to oppose the Nazis. Bonhoeffer was an important leader of the Confessional Church and he was also actively involved in opposing the Nazis within Germany. Bonhoeffer helped Jews to escape and he was also a courier, carrying secret messages from anti-Nazi groups. Eventually, he was arrested and tried by a court martial. No witnesses were allowed to support him and he was found guilty and sentenced to death. Dietrich Bonhoeffer was hanged at Flossenbürg concentration camp on 9 April 1945, just a month before the end of the war.

The Catholic Church

Hitler was aware that the Catholic Church was very powerful and as a 'world church' under the authority of the Pope, it was not so easy to control within Germany. The result was that on 8 July 1933, Hitler and the Pope signed an agreement called the **Concordat** (that is just another word for an agreement).

The Concordat stated that the Nazis would not interfere with the running of the Roman Catholic Church in Germany if the Church did not criticise the Nazis.

GLOSSARY

Concordat an agreement made between the Nazis and the Catholic Church in 1933

A member of the Catholic Church being saluted by Nazis

The Catholic Church did eventually speak out against Nazism, but why do photographs like this cause embarrassment to the Church?

The Catholic Church argued that they had no choice but to try to make a deal with the Nazis. Cardinal Faulhaber of Munich said 'With the Concordat we are hanged, without the Concordat we are hanged, drawn and quartered.' What he meant was that by making a deal with the Nazis, the Catholic Church faced criticism, but if they had not made the deal, the Nazis would have made life very difficult for the Catholic Church in Germany.

Attacks on the Catholic Church

The Nazis soon started to break their part of the Concordat. Catholic schools were closed and priests who spoke out against the Nazis were sent to concentration camps. Catholic magazines were censored and then banned, and Catholic youngsters were forced into joining the Hitler Youth.

Even before the Nazi persecution began, some Catholic bishops were very unhappy about Nazi policies and ideas. One example was the Nazi policy on euthanasia. The Nazis believed that physically and mentally handicapped people were not suitable to be included in the Nazi master race and should be killed. While euthanasia is a word that is sometimes translated as 'mercy killing', there was no mercy shown to Germany's disabled people. The Catholic Archbishop of Munster led a successful campaign to end the Nazi euthanasia policy of mentally disabled people.

By 1937 it was clear that the Nazis were ignoring the Concordat. The Pope then felt free to make public the Catholic Church's opposition to the Nazis and sent a message to all German parish priests to be read out in their churches. It was called 'With Burning Concern' and it attacked Hitler as 'a mad prophet' who was leading Germany to disaster.

The Nazis persecuted all religious groups

Jehovah's Witnesses are one example of a minority Christian sect that was persecuted by the Nazis. Since they were without important influence at home or abroad, it was possible to take more extreme measures against them than against the larger Christian churches. In particular, the Nazis were angered by the anti-military pacifism of these groups. Jehovah's Witnesses refused to do military service and resisted conscription. Any Jehovah's Witness caught by the Nazis was sent to a concentration camp, where many died.

Activity 1

Summarise this chapter

The following summary reminds you of what this chapter has been about. Words that are important in this chapter have been made into ANAGRAMS. Your task is to sort out the anagrams then write the correct version of this summary into your workbook or work file.

The Nazis tried to control the **CRASH IN IT** *churches in Germany. While the Nazis made an agreement called the* **NO CORD ACT** *with the Catholic Church, the Nazis tried to organise their own Protestant Church called the* **MANGER CRASH IN IT URCHCH**. *Protestant ministers who opposed the Nazis started the* **MANGER CONES LOAFS IN URCHCH**. *One of the leaders of that church was a famous anti-Nazi called* **TINRAM NO MIL REEL**.

Activity 2

The challenge! How far can you go?

The following questions go up in levels of difficulty in pairs. The first two are easy. The last two are hard. How many will you try to do?

1. Can you suggest another set of words for a Concordat?
2. Why was Hitler worried about the influence of the Christian churches in Germany?
3. Can you explain why the Confessional Church was started?
4. How would you summarise what Hitler did to control the Protestant Church in Germany?
5. Give arguments for and against the Concordat between the Catholic Church and the Nazi state.
6. Can you write more about the reasons why the Concordat broke down? Think about issues of what is right and wrong, and how morality and conscience made any agreement between the Church and the Nazis almost impossible to maintain.

Activity 3

Read Martin Niemöller's poem again.

- Rewrite it but this time replace the words communists, Jews and trade unionists with the names of persecuted groups that you have heard of nowadays. Although the names of persecuted groups have changed, has the meaning of the poem changed?
- Now update Niemöller's poem for a modern audience about a current issue involving injustice and public indifference. That means you must create a new version of Niemöller's message – it does not even have to be a poem. It could be a rap, a piece of performance art or a piece of artwork such as a painting. The only rule is that you must convey the feeling and meaning that Niemöller was trying to put across.

Question practice

National 4

Source A is from G. Puckett, writing in a Christian magazine.

SOURCE A

German Christians in Nazi Germany had a choice to make. Either they buried their beliefs or they stood up and declared that they could no longer approve of deplorable things. It was a difficult question for many – either to go with the flow or to stand up for their true beliefs.

Describe how Christians reacted to Nazi attempts to control their churches in the 1930s. You should use Source A and your own knowledge.

Success criteria

Include at least two facts explaining the reaction of Christians in Nazi Germany.

National 5

Source A is from a sermon given by Martin Niemöller on 27 June 1937.

SOURCE A

On Wednesday the secret police penetrated the closed church of Friedrich Werder and arrested at the altar eight members of Confessional Church. I think how yesterday at Saarbrucken six women and a trusted man of the Protestant community were arrested because they had circulated an election leaflet of the Confessional Church. And we recall today how the pulpit of St Anne's Church remains empty, because our pastor, with 47 other Christian brothers and sisters of our Protestant Church, has been taken into custody.

Evaluate the usefulness of Source A as evidence of the actions of the Nazi state to control the Christian Church. **(5 marks)**

This type of question has three possible ways to get marks.

The first way is to write about *who* wrote it, *when* and *why* it was written and to EXPLAIN WHY that information makes the source *more* or *less useful*. That's worth up to 4 marks.

For example, you could write, 'This source is useful as evidence because it is directly relevant to the question. The source is from a 1937 sermon given by Martin Niemöller. That suggests he is working within the Christian Church during the time of Nazi control of Germany.'

The second way is to focus on what is useful IN the source, in terms of what the question is asking. You need to find evidence from the source AND make a comment about how useful the evidence is for 1 mark. You can make up to two points and gain a maximum of 2 marks for this. You could write, 'The author – Martin Niemöller – describes how the Nazis were arresting members of the Confessional Church, which they disapproved of.' You should also find another piece of evidence showing examples of Nazi actions to control the Christian Church. Remember to add two quotes from the source to support your comments.

The third way is to write about what makes the source less than useful. Think about what could have been included which could have made the source more useful as evidence in terms of the question. This is worth up to 2 marks. For example, you could mention the new German Christian Church, which the Nazis approved of, and also the Concordat with the Catholic Church.

You could end by concluding that the source only gives a very one-sided, critical view of Nazi attempts to control the Christian Church.

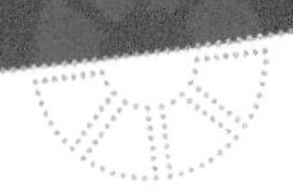

15 Jews in Nazi Germany

What is this chapter about?

Persecution of Jews is called anti-Semitism. All across Europe, for hundreds of years, Jewish people have been persecuted for being different. The purpose of anti-Semitic propaganda was to make Germans hate and fear Jews. Throughout the 1930s, Nazi persecution of the Jews in Germany increased and by the early 1940s, the Nazis' 'Final Solution' to 'the Jewish problem' was taking place, resulting in the mass murder of six million people.

By the end of this chapter you should be able to:

- Describe ways in which the Nazis persecuted Jewish people.
- Explain why persecution of the Jews was useful to the Nazis.

What was a Jew, according to the Nazis?

The Nazis defined exactly what a Jew was. In most countries, a Jew was simply a person who practised the religion of Judaism. In Nazi Germany, however, Jews were defined by their race, their blood and who their parents and grandparents were. If a person had at least three Jewish grandparents, then this person was purely of the Jewish race. A person was a 'half-Jew' if he or she had two Jewish grandparents. If a person had only one Jewish grandparent, the person was a 'quarter-Jew'. Quarter-Jews were less affected by the Nazi **persecution**, but pure Jews and half-Jews suffered the full force of Nazi discrimination.

GLOSSARY

Persecution picking on people or extreme bullying; mistreatment

Anti-Semitism hostility against Jews

Scapegoat something/someone to blame things on

Boycott refusing to use/buy something with the purpose of hurting the owner

Why were Jews persecuted?

At the time of the Nazi takeover in 1933, Jews made up less than one per cent of the German population. Nevertheless, Hitler exploited old feelings of **anti-Semitism** that were common in many countries in order to create a **scapegoat**. A scapegoat, in this sense, means an excuse to blame things on someone, in order to make yourself feel better because all your problems are someone else's fault.

According to Adolf Hitler, the Jews were responsible for everything that was wrong in Germany. In *Mein Kampf*, Hitler blamed them for losing the First World War. According to the Nazis, Jews were also responsible for Germany's economic crises and for plotting with Communists to take over Germany and eventually the world.

Hitler believed that pure Germans belonged to the Nordic, or north European, master race. Hitler called these true Germans Aryans and ideally they were tall, blonde and blue eyed. According to Hitler, Jews were polluting the Aryan master race.

How were Jews persecuted?

Immediately after the elections to the *Reichstag* on 5 March 1933, the persecution of the Jews began. Jewish people were attacked, some even killed, and Jewish businesses were harassed or destroyed.

The first obvious anti-Jewish policy was the **boycott** of Jewish stores that started on 1 April 1933. Nazi Brownshirts stood outside Jewish shops to stop Germans from using them.

By 1934, all Jewish shops were marked with the yellow Star of David or had the word ***Juden*** written on the window. Then a wave of new laws was introduced. On buses, trains and park benches, Jews had to sit on seats marked specifically for them.

Non-Jewish children at schools were taught to hate and persecute Jews. Teachers humiliated Jewish school children. When Jewish children were bullied at school nothing happened to the bullies. If the Jewish children then started to avoid going to school, Nazi propaganda claimed that Jewish children were lazy and could not be bothered to attend.

An SA member standing outside a Jewish-owned shop reminding each would-be shopper of the boycott slogan: 'Germans protect yourselves. Do not buy from Jews.'

A cartoon from a children's primary school book. It shows a wealthy Jewish man trying to abduct a young German girl by offering her cheap jewellery.

If this poster was made today about child safety, what slogan would you put on it to make your message clear?

How did the Nuremberg Laws make life very difficult for Jews?

In 1935, the Nuremberg Laws were passed. Hitler wanted to make life so unpleasant for Jews in Germany that they would emigrate. Jewish emigration certainly did increase after the laws on citizenship and race were passed. Those that could pay a fine were allowed to leave the country. Approximately 300,000 of Germany's 500,000 Jews left the country between 1933 and 1941 before emigration was halted.

For those Jews who could not afford to escape from Germany, life became increasingly difficult. Many shops refused to sell food to them. Medicines were also difficult to get hold of as chemists would not sell to Jewish people.

Most important of all, the new rule stated that Jews could no longer be citizens of Germany. That meant they did not have the protection of the law and they were not even allowed to have official papers or passports.

During the 1936 Berlin Olympics the persecution of the Jews was relaxed. Once the world's cameras and newspaper reporters had left, however, the anti-Jewish violence started up again and reached a peak in 1938 with ***Kristallnacht***: the 'night of the broken glass'.

GLOSSARY

Juden German word for Jews

Kristallnacht an organised attack on Jews across Germany on the night of 9–10 November 1938

What was *Kristallnacht*?

Kristallnacht was an organised attack on the Jews of Germany on the night of 9–10 November 1938.

Ten thousand shops owned by Jews were destroyed and their contents stolen. Four hundred **synagogues** were burnt down. Homes and synagogues were set on fire and left to burn. Ninety-one Jews were killed and around 20,000 were sent to concentration camps.

The literal translation of *Kristallnacht* is 'crystal night', so-named because of the amount of broken glass lying in the streets of Germany's cities the next morning.

Despite the huge amount of damage done to Jewish property, the Jewish community was ordered to pay a one billion mark fine for all the damage and the clearing up afterwards.

Kristallnacht, 1938. A burning synagogue.

Why did *Kristallnacht* happen?

The Nazis claimed the attacks were just the natural reaction of the German people on hearing the news that a Jew in Paris had killed a German official. Minister of Propaganda Joseph Goebbels wrote, 'The outbreak of fury by the people on the night of 9–10 November was neither organised nor prepared but broke out spontaneously.' The evidence presents a different story.

An American eyewitness wrote at the time that when the local people woke the next morning and saw the shattered shop windows, looted stores and destroyed Jewish homes, they were obviously shocked and left puzzled over what had happened.

GLOSSARY

Synagogues Jewish places of worship

Later, official orders about *Kristallnacht* were found. A Nazi official called Reinhard Heydrich sent a message entitled 'Instructions for measures against Jews on 10 November 1938' in which he wrote:

Demonstrations against the Jews are to be expected in all parts of the Reich *in the course of the coming night, 9–10 November 1938. Synagogues are to be burnt down as long as the fires will not threaten neighbouring buildings. Places of business and apartments belonging to Jews may be destroyed but not looted. Care is to be taken that non-Jewish businesses are completely protected against damage. The demonstrations against Jews are not to be prevented by the police. As many Jews as possible in all districts, especially the rich, are to be arrested.*

A poster for the 1939 Nazi propaganda film The Eternal Jew. *This was all part of the continuing process of making Jews seem less than human. In the film, scenes of Jewish home life are mixed with film of hundreds of rats.*

From persecution to genocide

Kristallnacht was the most organised attempt so far to persecute Jews in Nazi Germany, but it was to get much worse.

By 1939, the desire of the Nazis to wipe out the Jews of Germany was clear. On 31 October 1939, a leading Nazi called Julius Streicher declared, 'The victory will be only entirely and finally achieved when the whole world is free of Jews.'

During the Second World War, the Nazis developed the technology to murder millions of Jews in Europe. At a meeting in December 1941, Hans Frank, Nazi governor of Poland, said, 'Gentlemen, we must annihilate the Jews wherever we find them and wherever it is possible …' This marked the beginning of the Final Solution, the Nazis' attempt to annihilate the entire Jewish population of Europe, an estimated 11 million people.

What had started as persecution evolved into a policy of **genocide**. Genocide means a deliberate attempt to wipe out an entire race of people. The Nazis also murdered gypsies, Jehovah's Witnesses, Communists, homosexuals, and the mentally and physically disabled. However, the Nazis did not try to wipe out these groups. Only the Jews were to be destroyed completely. The suffering of the Jewish people and other groups persecuted by the Nazis did not end until Allied armies defeated the Nazis in 1945. Only then did the Nazi dictatorship collapse. Nazi Germany was at an end.

GLOSSARY

Genocide the deliberate wiping out (annihilation) of an entire race of people

How do the images in this chapter show the escalation (increase) in persecution of Jews in the 1930s? Why do you think the Nazi state wanted Jews to appear as non-German, even non-human and life-threatening monsters?

Yellow Stars of David had to be worn by Jews after 1939 to identify them as different from 'proper' Germans

Activity 1

Summarise this chapter

The following summary reminds you of what this chapter has been about. Words that are important in this chapter have been made into ANAGRAMS. Your task is to sort out the anagrams then write the correct version of this summary into your workbook or work file.

SWEJ in Germany were **PET RESCUED** as soon as the Nazis came to power. It started with a **TO COT BY** of Jewish shops but got worse with the **URN BERG ME SLAW**. In 1938 **STILL HACK L RANT** showed how the Nazis were planning to attack Jews all across Germany. The Nazis' final solution to what they called 'the Jewish problem' was **NIECE DOG**.

Activity 2

The challenge! How far can you go?

The following questions go up in levels of difficulty in pairs. The first two are easy. The last two are hard. How many will you try to do?

1 Can you suggest another set of words for disliking Jews?
2 Why were the Jews persecuted in Nazi Germany?

3 Can you explain what the Nuremberg Laws were?
4 How would you summarise what happened on *Kristallnacht*?

5 Can you come up with a theory why the vast majority of Germans did nothing to stop the persecution of the Jews? Your answer should be thoughtful and developed with several different strands of thought.
6 What would you say is the importance of knowing about the Nazis' treatment of Jews?

Activity 3

Your task now is to write an 'explain' question about the growth of anti-Semitism in Germany in the 1930s.

Explain questions often start like this: 'Explain the reasons why …'

To successfully answer this type of question you must give six reasons why something happened, so your question must allow someone to make that same number of points in the answer.

Next you must make up a mark scheme to help someone mark the answer. List the points you would expect to see in a good answer. This will indicate whether you have allowed for a wide-enough question. This question is worth 6 marks, so you must include at least six or more points in your mark scheme to allow for other people to use slightly different material in their answers.

Now partner up with a friend who has also written their own 'explain' question and answer. Swap so that you can attempt to write an answer to their question while they have a go at answering yours.

After ten minutes, stop writing. Swap the work back with your partner so that she or he can mark your answer while you mark theirs.

Question practice

National 4

Source A was written by a recent historian about the persecution of Jews in Nazi Germany.

SOURCE A

The first direct action taken was to boycott Jewish shops. Nazi papers screamed their hatred of Jews and then the Nuremberg Laws turned Jews into non-Germans. They lost the rights they had been born with. It was a disgrace.

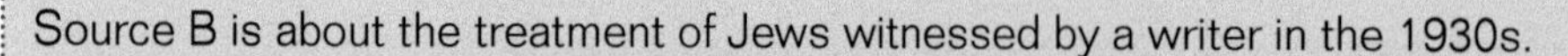

Source B is about the treatment of Jews witnessed by a writer in the 1930s.

SOURCE B

Yes, of course, we saw that Jews were picked on, that life was difficult for them. But was it not their own fault? We worked hard but Jews always seemed to be richer, have better jobs. We were not Jews so why should we care what happened to them?

Compare the views in Source A and Source B about the treatment of Jews. Describe in detail their similarities and/or differences. You can also briefly compare the overall attitude of the sources.

Success criteria

- Examine the two sources in order to show two simple points of comparison or develop one point of similarity or difference.
- An example of a simple comparison is: 'Source A says … and Source B says …'.
- An example of a developed comparison is : 'Sources A and B disagree about the treatment of the Jews. Source A says … and Source B says …'.

National 5

This is a 'how fully' question. In this type of question you need to select the points from the source which are relevant to the question. Usually there will be three points in the source. Then, to get full marks, you need to bring in points from recall that are also relevant to the question which haven't been mentioned in the source. Finally, you MUST make a judgement about the fullness (or completeness) of the source as an explanation, otherwise you can only achieve a maximum of 2 marks.

Source A is from a letter written by Lady Rumbold, the wife of the British Ambassador in Germany. In it she describes what she saw on the morning after *Kristallnacht*.

SOURCE A

The main streets of the city were a positive litter of shattered plate glass. All of the synagogues were irreparably gutted by flames. One of the largest clothing stores was destroyed. No attempts on the part of the fire brigade were made to extinguish the fire. It is extremely difficult to believe, but the owners of the clothing store were actually charged with setting the fire and on that basis were dragged from their beds at 6 a.m. and clapped into prison and many male German Jews have been sent to concentration camps.

Assess how fully Source A describes the persecution of Jews in Nazi Germany in the 1930s. (6 marks)

In terms of this question, you need to think about how fully the letter describes the persecution of Jews throughout the 1930s. You should mention the different examples of attacks on Jews on *Kristallnacht* as reported by Lady Rumbold, but that will only score 3 marks. For a further 3 marks you must think of other examples of anti-Jewish persecution used in Nazi Germany but not mentioned in the source. For example, you might want to think about boycotts and the Nuremberg Laws.

Please do not write information about the Holocaust. The question asks about persecution of Jews in the 1930s and the Holocaust is a term used specifically to mean the mass murder of Jews during the Second World War, which did not start until 1939. The Holocaust began in 1941 approximately.

SECTION 4

Nazi social and economic policies

16 Feeling good about being Nazi: the Nazis and propaganda

What is this chapter about?

Propaganda means controlling information to make people think and behave in a certain way. The Nazis had total control over all sources of information such as cinema, newspapers and radio. Propaganda could take many forms; it could be exaggerated stories or rumours to make people dislike groups of people that the Nazis did not approve of. It could also be biased or, in many cases, completely made-up stories or reports to make people like the Nazis and maintain loyalty to them.

By the end of this chapter you should be able to:

- Describe examples of Nazi propaganda.
- Explain why propaganda was so important to the Nazis.

Why was propaganda important to the Nazis?

Nazi propaganda was an important tool to establish and keep control of the population. Evidence that went against the Nazi message was censored. The Nazis discouraged any discussion of different points of view. Since the Nazis had total control over access to information, it was hard for ordinary Germans to see, hear or read any anti-Nazi views. Germans were told what to think – or were they?

In fact, recent research by historians suggests that propaganda did not really persuade people to believe something they did not want to believe. Educated middle-class Germans accepted Nazi propaganda because it told them something they already wanted to believe – that Hitler was saving Germany, that the Jews were wicked, that Germany had not really lost the First World War and so on. The genius of effective propaganda is that it directs people's thoughts to where you want them to go.

Hitler knew that effective propaganda had to be simple, so easily remembered slogans were used repeatedly. Hitler wrote: 'The intelligence of the masses is small. Their forgetfulness is great. They must be told the same thing a thousand times.'

Who was Joseph Goebbels?

Joseph Goebbels was the man in charge of spreading the Nazi message across Germany. In the late 1920s and early 1930s Goebbels worked hard at persuading Germans to vote for the Nazis. Once Hitler became *Führer*, Goebbels had the job of convincing Germans that they liked living in a Nazi dictatorship.

The Ministry of Popular Enlightenment and Propaganda was created to organise all Nazi propaganda. The core of much Nazi propaganda was that to be a good German, one had to be a good Nazi. Goebbels said, 'It is the task of state propaganda to simplify complicated ways of thinking so that even the smallest man in the street may understand.' Goebbels did not add that he also saw it as his job to censor or prevent Germans seeing or reading any anti-Nazi viewpoint. In May 1933, Goebbels even organised a book-burning campaign where 'good Germans' were encouraged to throw books disapproved of by the Nazis on to huge bonfires.

If you were in charge of propaganda now, how would you update Goebbels' statement in the caption to the twenty-first century?

Joseph Goebbels, the man in charge of Nazi propaganda. He said, 'The radio will be to the twentieth century what the press was to the nineteenth.'

Propaganda and the radio

In the 1930s, radio and newspapers were the only ways that the outside world could get into people's homes. The Nazis were well aware of the power of radio. By 1939 over 70 per cent of German homes had a radio. This was the highest ownership of radios in the world at that time. But it was no accident that so many German homes had radios. The Nazis produced millions of cheap radios that could only receive Nazi radio stations.

GLOSSARY

Joseph Goebbels the man in charge of propaganda in Nazi Germany

Aryan the German ideal of a north European, blonde-haired, blue-eyed master race

How important was Hitler to the Nazi propaganda machine?

Hitler was the star that most Germans wanted to see and hear. Before his speeches, Hitler rehearsed carefully, even practising the way he would stand and how he would use his arms. He manipulated crowds, often arriving late and then standing in front of them, silent for a few minutes. By doing so Hitler increased the tension. He often started slowly, but as he continued, he became louder and faster as if speaking with great conviction and emotion. In this way, he connected with the inner fears and hopes of each person listening to him.

Hitler's speeches were like spell-binding performances to his audiences. Hitler also knew the importance of keeping his speeches simple. He repeated the main points again and again and used humour and anger to drive his audiences wild with enthusiasm.

How were the Olympic Games of 1936 used as Nazi propaganda?

The 1936 Berlin Olympic Games were the perfect opportunity for Hitler and Goebbels to show the world how powerful the **Aryan** 'master race' really was. The games were shown in a very famous film called *Olympia* by the German film director Leni Riefenstahl.

During the games, the anti-Semitic posters that had been very common in Germany were removed. Signs that stated 'Jews not welcome here' were taken down.

Hitler leading the German army in a poster entitled 'Long live Germany'

Both those pictures using the image of Hitler are examples of propaganda. Can you explain what messages they are trying to give about Hitler?

Advertising a British song called 'Adolf'. The song was a big wartime hit.

Hitler wanted to show the world's press and media how the members of his 'master race' were world-beaters. To keep up the racially pure image, the chief of police arrested all Roma people (gypsies) and kept them in a nearby concentration camp, sandwiched between a cemetery and a sewage dump, during the games.

The Berlin Olympics were a huge public relations triumph for the Nazis.

The huge Olympic stadium was completed on time and held 100,000 spectators. In comparison, the London 2012 Olympic Stadium held 80,000. Total ticket revenues made a profit of over one million marks. It was the first time that the Olympic torch was carried between Greece and the host nation. The games were also the first to have live television coverage. The pictures went to special viewing rooms throughout Berlin and a few private TV sets.

Famous myths

Germany's athletic superstar of the time was Luz Long, a brilliant long-jumper who easily fitted into the Nazi image of the blonde-haired, blue-eyed master race superiority. However, the real hero of the games was Jesse Owens, an African American and therefore, according to Nazi master race ideology, inferior to the German athletes.

Owens is best known for winning four gold medals. A common **myth** is that Hitler was so angry that a black man won that he refused to present the medals. It's not true. Hitler *did* leave the stadium early when a black athlete won a gold medal, but it was not Owens. Hitler simply was not present when Owens won his medals.

GLOSSARY

Myth something that is believed to be true by lots of people but is really untrue

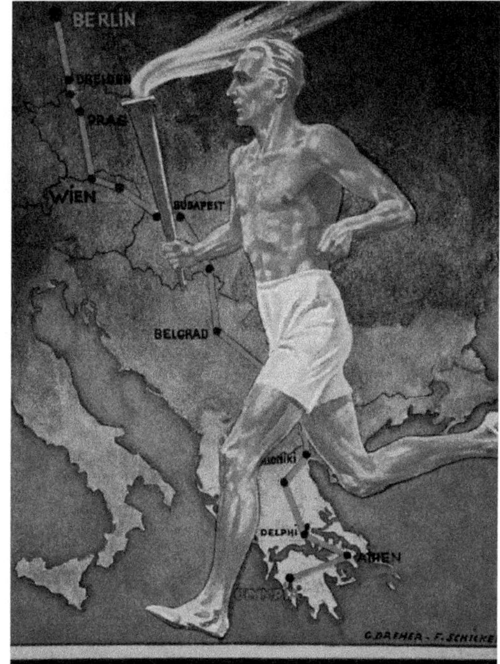

'Torch relay from Olympia to Berlin.' A poster advertising the 1936 Olympic Games.

Why were the Nuremberg rallies important to the Nazis?

A Nazi rally had been held every year at the city of Nuremberg since 1923. Once Hitler came to power the Nuremberg rallies became huge propaganda events showing off Nazi power.

Officially, the Nazis called the rallies the National Congress of the Party of the German People. The name suggests a strong link between the Nazi Party and all the German people. Each year, the rallies got bigger and by the late 1930s there were over half a million people taking part. Hundreds of thousands of people attended these rallies, which could be likened to huge religious ceremonies or rock concerts.

The crowds were dazzled by vast displays of athletic strength and military power. The gatherings were so big that mock battles with tanks and aircraft were staged for the spectators. As night fell, torch-lit parades and the use of sound, light and smoke created a magical atmosphere that worked the crowd up into a frenzy. The sight of Nazi symbols and flags filled visitors' eyes and thundering drums and blaring trumpets filled their ears. Then the cheering began.

Hitler would keep the crowd waiting but when he appeared like a god, everyone went wild. He started speaking quietly and slowly. The crowd hung on his every word. He promised a 1000-year empire and a brave new world led by the German master race. As he continued, he became more exaggerated and theatrical. Hitler drove the crowd into an emotional frenzy. The people loved it. They chanted and roared their approval.

How many words can you think of that would describe what the Nazis wanted to achieve by organising huge propaganda events such as the rallies?

Did the rallies have another purpose?

The rallies also gave Hitler a chance to show off his military power. At the rallies, the German people could gaze in amazement at pretend battles in giant arenas. Marches with flags, drums and uniformed men and women displayed the militarism of the Nazi state. Militarism means to build up respect for the armed forces – the military – and to create a belief that it is normal to increase the power of the army and to plan for war. Militarism relied on propaganda and indoctrination to convince people that Germany should arm itself in readiness for war, only 15 years after the slaughter of the First World War.

A photograph of part of a Nuremberg rally

Just like the Olympics, the Nuremberg rallies were turned into a movie by Leni Riefenstahl, called *Triumph of the Will*. It is still available today because of its brilliant film-making skills. The film is especially impressive when it shows the huge size of the German military machine.

Foreign visitors were dazzled and rather afraid of the sheer size of the German military. How could it have got so strong? How could any foreign power stand up against the Nazis? In reality, some of the military equipment on show at the rallies was fake. Carefully painted cardboard outlines of tanks were placed on top of small cars that raced around the arena. When the rallies made light shows out of hundreds of searchlights firing pillars of light skywards, little did the audience know that those displays used every single searchlight in Germany.

Propaganda, either in films or posters, rallies or the Olympic Games, were all used for the same purpose: to make people believe that life was so much better under the Nazis, and for many people it was.

Activity 1

Summarise this chapter

The following summary reminds you of what this chapter has been about. Words that are important in this chapter have been made into ANAGRAMS. Your task is to sort out the anagrams then write the correct version of this summary into your workbook or work file.

PHEJOS BOB GLEES was in charge of Nazi **PANDAGROAP**. Germans were told that **RAYANS** were a master race and all other people were inferior. Nazis used many methods including **FLIM AS ANDROID** to spread propaganda. Big occasions such as the **POLY MERLIN BICS** and the annual **EMBERS RAIL LEG RUN** were perfect opportunities to show the world how good the Nazi state was.

Activity 2

If this is the answer what is the question?

Below you will find a list of words or names. You have to make up a question that can only be answered by the word on the list. For example, if the word 'Owens' was the answer, a question could be 'What was the last name of the American gold medal winning runner whose first name was Jesse?'

Here is your list of answers:

- propaganda
- Goebbels
- rallies
- 100,000
- 1936
- Aryan
- Berlin
- Nuremberg
- military.

Activity 3

Your task is to design a hanging mobile (such as one used in a child's bedroom) illustrating examples of Nazi propaganda. Since it is for a child, the best examples would be positive and brightly coloured. In practical terms, the best structure is usually two criss-crossing wire coat-hangers.

Make at least four big smiley faces. In the middle of each face (or hanging directly below) show an example of positive propaganda encouraging people to support the Nazis.

Remember, your mobile must be clearly readable from a distance. Your mobile is most likely to be looked at from below or the side, so think where you will place your items. Use your imagination and adapt the suggestions here to do what you think would be appropriate.

See page 47 for other helpful tips on how on how to complete this activity.

Question practice

National 4

Source A is about the effect of Nazi propaganda on people in Germany in 1936. It quotes Myra Strachan, who was on holiday in Germany and went to the Berlin Olympics.

SOURCE A

Until then I had never really experienced the power of Nazism. Flags and posters and huge Nazi statues were everywhere. I felt that Germany must be a great and powerful country.

Arthur Marwick, *Women at War*, Fontana, 1977.

Give reasons to explain why the Nazis thought propaganda was so important. You should use Source A and your own knowledge.

Success criteria

Provide at least two pieces of information explaining the effect of Nazi propaganda.

National 5

Source A describes Hitler speaking at a Nazi rally.

SOURCE A

When Hitler stepped onto the platform there was not a sound to be heard. Then he began to speak, quietly at first. Before long however his voice had risen to a hoarse shriek that gave an extraordinary effect. He was holding the crowd, and me, under his hypnotic spell. I don't know how to describe the emotions that swept over me as I listened to this man. When he spoke of the disgrace of Versailles, I felt ready to jump on any enemy.

Kurt Ludecke, *I Knew Hitler*, Jarrolds, 1938.

Source B also describes Hitler speaking at a Nazi rally.

SOURCE B

When Hitler moved onto the stage 100,000 people became silent. Hitler started his speech very quietly. People had to strain to hear him. By the end however he was yelling at the crowd and the crowd yelled back. Hitler spoke of how awful the Treaty of Versailles was and of the need to tear it up. The crowd were hypnotised by Hitler. When he finished, the audience rose and cheered and cheered.

Compare the views of Source A and Source B about Hitler as a speaker. **(4 marks)**

This question is worth 4 marks and you can get full marks by making two fully supported comparisons, which means you state what the disagreement or agreement is and quote from the sources to support the point you are making. Another way to get marks is if you identify all the points of agreements or disagreements in the sources briefly.

This is a comparison question so remember that the skill being assessed is your ability to compare. It does not mean your ability to describe two sources.

You will not gain marks for writing simply 'Source A says …' and then 'Source B says …' You must always explain the point you are making by using your own words. This is called a developed comparison. One way to do that is to write, 'Source A says … and then Source B says … This shows that the opinions about Hitler as a speaker agree/disagree because …'

17 Hitler and the youth of Germany

What is this chapter about?

Young Germans were taught in schools to be good Nazis. Out of school, youth organisations continued the work of turning Germany's youth into supporters of Hitler. Hitler planned to control the thoughts and actions of all of Germany's youth. In order to do that, he controlled what was taught in schools and what children did in their leisure time. Hitler's aim was to indoctrinate Germany's children. By turning the youth of Germany into obedient Nazis who never questioned Hitler's authority and ideas, Hitler could guarantee generations of future support.

By the end of this chapter you should be able to:

- Describe how Hitler tried to turn the youth of Germany into true Nazis.
- Explain why Hitler put such importance on education and leisure activities for Germany's youth.

What does indoctrinate mean?

Hitler wanted to brainwash or **indoctrinate** all of Germany's children to make them grow up as good Nazi supporters. A German child at school during the 1930s remembered, 'we were programmed to think as Nazis', and that was the main aim of the Nazi education system.

GLOSSARY

Indoctrination making people believe and think what you want them to

Throughout the education of Germany's children, Nazi indoctrination was ever-present. By controlling every aspect of education, the Nazis hoped to create a generation of unthinking, obedient Nazis ready and willing to continue Hitler's dream of building a 1000-year Reich (empire). When Hitler was asked about adults who disagreed with him he said, 'Your child belongs to us already.'

Many people think this is a very frightening photograph. Do you agree or not? Why do you think that?

This photo was taken in 1938. The girl is about 12 years of age.

Reorganising schools

Hitler appointed **Bernhard Rust** as head of the Nazi education system and his first aim was to remove as many anti-Nazi teachers as possible. Any teacher who spoke out against the Nazi regime was sacked, so most teachers taught what they were told to teach. All school textbooks had to be approved by the Nazi authorities.

As the children became older, school subjects such as history, biology and languages all emphasised the importance of Germany and the German people and the inferiority of other races. Nazi education aimed to make children physically fit, to make them believe that the Aryan race was superior to all others and to learn how great Germany had been in the past. For example, chemistry lessons focused on developing a knowledge of chemical warfare and explosives, while maths problems usually involved using maths in a military and aggressive way such as this:

A Panzer tank carries 1000 litres of fuel and consumes 500 litres per 100 km. What is the furthest target a Panzer could reach to attack and then return to base without refuelling?

Specialist schools were created to train Nazi Germany's future leaders. They were called *Napolas* (National Political Institutes of Education) and were run by the SS. To get into *Napolas*, students had to be true Aryans, physically fit and members of the Hitler Youth.

When students left school at 18 they had to spend six months in the German labour service before some went to university. Universities also came under Nazi control. Girls were not encouraged to go to university. In 1933 there were over 18,000 women in German universities but by 1939 there were fewer than 6000. All Jews were expelled and people with anti-Nazi views were also forced out.

GLOSSARY

Bernhard Rust head of German education

Krupp's a German company making very strong steel

Hitler Jugend Hitler Youth, a paramilitary group for German boys

Out of school: the youth organisations

Nazi education schemes were only part of the plan to create the next generation of Nazi supporters. The other part of the plan involved creating youth organisations for Germany's youth. There were separate organisations for boys and girls. The task of the boys' section was to prepare them for military service. For girls, the organisation prepared them for motherhood.

Hitler said, 'The weak must be chiselled away. I want young men and women who can suffer pain. A young German must be as swift as a greyhound, as tough as leather, and as hard as **Krupp's** steel. There must be nothing weak and gentle about it. That is how I will create the New Order.'

The Hitler Youth had been created in the 1920s. By 1933, its membership stood at 100,000. After Hitler came to power, all other youth movements were abolished. As a result, the Hitler Youth grew quickly, with membership reaching over two million by the end of 1933.

This photograph was taken at a Hitler Youth rally at Nuremberg in 1938

How were boys trained?

Boys first joined the 'Little Fellows' organisation at six years old and stayed until they were ten. They did mainly outdoor sports-type activities such as hiking, rambling and camping. Between the ages of 10 and 13 boys were members of the German Young People. At the age of 13 they transferred to the ***Hitler Jugend*** (HJ) until the age of 18.

In the HJ, boys learned military skills such as marching, using a bayonet, grenade throwing, trench digging, map reading, how to get under barbed wire and pistol shooting. In 1937, a Hitler Youth rifle school was also established. About 1.5 million boys were trained in rifle shooting and military field exercises over the next few years. There were also tests to see if they had learned about Nazism and all boys who passed the test were given a special **dagger** marked 'Blood and Honour'.

GLOSSARY

Dagger a small knife designed for fighting

It is easy for us to disapprove of the Hitler Youth, but try to imagine how you would have felt if you were a German teenager in 1936. Think what the Hitler Youth offered and how Hitler seemed to be making Germany a strong powerful country once again. Would you have joined the HJ or the League of German Maidens?

How were girls trained?

In 1934, Hitler said in a speech, 'for a woman, her world is her husband, her family, her children and her home', and that summed up Nazi attitudes to the education of girls.

Girls aged 10–14 years joined the Young Maidens where they were taught how to become good mothers and housewives. Housekeeping skills, health and nutrition were all part of the girls' education, as was maintaining a healthy body for later child bearing. Girls had to be able to run 60 metres in 14 seconds, throw a ball 12 metres, complete a two-hour march, swim 100 metres and know how to make a bed.

Girls aged 14–21 joined the League of German Maidens where they were further prepared for their roles as mothers of future Germans. Once true Aryan girls grew up to be mothers they could look forward to winning the 'Mother's Cross': bronze for having four children, silver for six and gold for eight.

Martha Dodd, who lived in Germany in the 1930s, saw what had happened to young German girls and women. In her book, *My Years in Germany* (Gollancz, 1939) she wrote:

Young girls from the age of ten onwards were taken into organisations where they were taught only two things: to take care of their bodies so they could bear as many children as the state needed and to be loyal to National Socialism [Nazism]. Birth control information is frowned on and practically forbidden. Women have been deprived of all rights except that of childbirth and hard work in the home.

'Youth serves the Führer.' A Nazi poster from about 1936.

The posters and the rally photograph are examples of Nazi propaganda trying to persuade young Germans to join the Hitler Youth movement. Do you think they are effective adverts for the Hitler Youth movement? Why?

'All 10-year-olds [come] to us.' A Nazi poster from about 1936.

Were people forced to join?

At first, membership of the Hitler Youth organisations was voluntary, but in 1936, membership of the HJ was made compulsory for all boys aged 15 to 18. At the same time, all other youth organisations were banned. However, even by 1938, attendance at Hitler Youth meetings was so poor – barely 25 per cent – that the authorities decided to tighten up attendance with a new law. On 25 March 1939, parents were warned that unless children attended HJ meetings regularly they would be forcibly removed from their parents and placed in the custody of state-run orphanages.

Most members of the Hitler Youth joined the organisation because they thought it was fun and exciting. One HJ member said:

I think most of the other boys joined for the reason I did. They were looking for a place where they could get together with other boys in exciting activities. There was no direct or obvious political indoctrination ... We did march in parades ... we enjoyed ourselves and felt important.

Another member of the HJ explained:

All my friends had these black shorts and brown shirts and a swastika and a little dagger which said Blood and Honour. I wanted it just like everybody else. I wanted to belong. These were my schoolmates.

By 1939 the Hitler Youth claimed to have 7.3 million members, making it the largest youth organisation in the world.

Activity 1

Summarise this chapter

The following summary reminds you of what this chapter has been about. Words that are important in this chapter have been made into ANAGRAMS. Your task is to sort out the anagrams then write the correct version of this summary into your workbook or work file.

In schools, young Germans were taught to be good Nazis. Out-of-school youth organisations such as the **TIL HER NED JUG** and the **GEL AUE** of **MANGER ADMEN IS** continued the work of turning Germany's youth into supporters of Hitler. Boys were trained for **AIR MY LIT** service while the focus of girls' education was to turn them into good **HO TERMS** of the future master race.

Activity 2

Work in pairs. In this activity, make up at least ten questions that you would use to test someone's knowledge about Nazi education and youth organisations in Nazi Germany.

To make up the questions, first work out what you want to ask. You must have a clear idea of what answer you want for your question.

This activity is different from earlier activities that look the same. Those activities asked about understanding. Therefore, there were lots of 'explain' type questions.

This activity is to help you check your knowledge. Questions that start as 'Who was ...' or 'Describe ...' or 'How did ...' are all suitable. Try to make a mixture of 'big' and 'small' questions. A big question could be 'How did the Nazis try to control young people in Germany?' A small question could be 'What was a *Napola*?'

You can arrange for answers to be spoken or written, but in both cases answers should be presented in proper sentences.

Your questions should be mature and well presented. The purpose is to help learning, not to catch people out with really tricky questions.

When you have both completed ten questions, try them out on each other. Can your partner answer your question? And can you answer your partner's question in exchange? Can you each make up five more questions based around the information your partner did not know?

Activity 3

Redesign your curriculum!

Your history course is part of the Curriculum for Excellence. The Nazis wanted to create a curriculum for Aryan excellence!

List all the subjects you do. Think of the sorts of things you do in each different subject. Now imagine you were involved in schools in Nazi Germany. How could you redesign the content, skills and assessment of each subject so that they match up with Nazi aims?

Write your new curriculum as a list of subjects. Beside each subject explain not only what you have changed but also how the change matches up with Nazi policy.

Question practice

National 4

Source A is by Adolf Hitler.

SOURCE A

I am beginning with the young. Look at my magnificent youngsters! Are there finer ones anywhere in the world? Look at these young men and boys! What material! With them I can make a new world.

Describe how Hitler tried to train the Hitler Youth to become good Nazis. You should use Source A and your own knowledge.

Success criteria

Write at least two points of information, or one developed point, on how the Hitler Youth were trained to become good Nazis.

National 5

Source A is by Marianne MacKinnon, who remembers going to school in Nazi Germany during the 1930s.

SOURCE A

School changed a lot. We never questioned the new books and the new subjects which appeared. The number of physical education (PE) periods was increased at the expense of religious instruction. Less studious pupils, like myself, were positively delighted when competitive games were introduced. I loved the physical fitness programme. An hour spent in the gym was infinitely preferable to sweating over arithmetic. I was less keen on the loud Nazi songs we had to sing.

Source B is about education in Nazi Germany.

SOURCE B

The normal timetable allocation of PE periods was increased to five by 1938. This was instead of religious instruction. PE gained higher status as a subject and there was serious suggestion that the PE instructor in every school should automatically be appointed deputy headmaster. Something else new was the introduction of subjects like racial studies. Weekly morning assemblies became Nazi ceremonies where hymns were replaced with Nazi songs. Education was considered important by the Nazis.

Compare the views of Source A and Source B about changes in education made by the Nazis. (4 marks)

As stated on page 90, with 'compare' questions, you are being asked to demonstrate whether you think the sources agree or not. The skill being assessed is your ability to compare. This does not mean your ability to describe two sources.

You will not gain marks for writing simply 'Source A says …' and then 'Source B says …' You must always explain the point you are making by using your own words. This is called a developed comparison. One way to do this is to write, 'Source A says … and then Source B says … This shows that the opinions about the changes in education agree/disagree because …'

The question is worth 4 marks so try to make four different connections between the sources.

18 Germany's economic miracle: was it for real?

What is this chapter about?

For most Germans, Hitler provided huge improvements in their lives – or at least, so they were told. One of the big propaganda claims of the Nazis was that they solved Germany's economic problems. Just like today, the main worries of people were based on jobs and prices and their standard of living. How true was it that Nazi economic policies made life better for most Germans?

By the end of this chapter you should be able to:

- Describe how Hitler made most Germans feel good about living in a Nazi state.
- Explain why historians think the Nazi economic miracle was not as good as it seemed.

The Nazi economic miracle?

If you had been a German in 1936 how would you have felt? Worried? Afraid? Scared? Or would you have felt happy? Positive? Confident?

The words happy and positive are not words usually linked to Nazi Germany, but stop and think about it a little more.

Hitler and the Nazis came to power in the middle of the Great Depression. They knew that it would be very difficult to rule if the majority of the German people were against them. That is why the Nazis provided positive images of Nazism and deliberately created big national events such as the Berlin Olympics and the Nuremberg rallies to create a **'feel-good factor'** that made most Germans feel positive about their new government.

GLOSSARY

'Feel-good factor' when the population of a country feel cheerful and politicians can take advantage of that to gain support

Autobahn the German motorway system

How did Hitler make most Germans feel good about living in the new Nazi state?

The most important change was that everybody had a job and a wage. To people who had been unemployed and starving, 'work and bread' was well worth the price of losing a democratic government with civil liberties.

Hitler began a huge programme of public works including planting forests, and building hospitals and schools. He also built public buildings such as the 1936 Olympic Stadium. The construction of the ***autobahns*** created work for 80,000 men. At the same time, rearmament created jobs in the armaments industry.

The streets were safe and there was almost no crime. Nazi rallies provided excitement and fun. Nazi youth groups provided activities and holidays for young people. On the surface, Nazi policies seemed to be working and the standard of living got better for many Germans. For most Germans, 'getting better' meant secure jobs, rising wages and a better standard of living. As long as life seemed to get better, most Germans were prepared to go along with the Nazis, even if they did not agree with their actions or ideology.

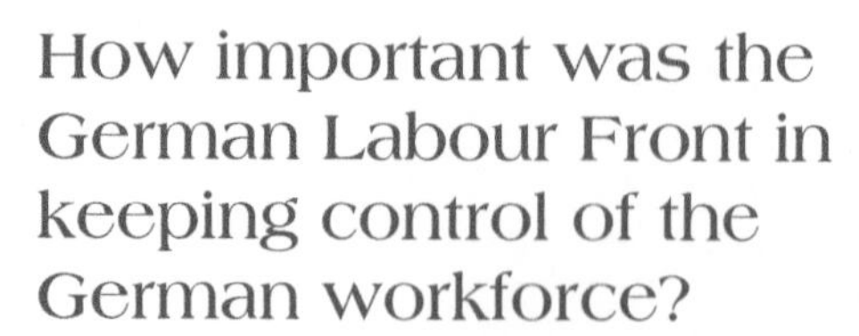

How important was the German Labour Front in keeping control of the German workforce?

The German Labour Front, known as DAF, was a Nazi organisation that tried to include and control all German workers. It was organised by Robert Ley and, at first, it sounds a bit threatening but as part of DAF, workers were given wages and security of work – it was almost impossible to be sacked or laid off. Workers benefited from social security and leisure programmes. They had regular breaks and regular working hours.

How does this poster suggest that Nazism is good for Germany? Can you think of any modern-day examples in which similar images are used to advertise something?

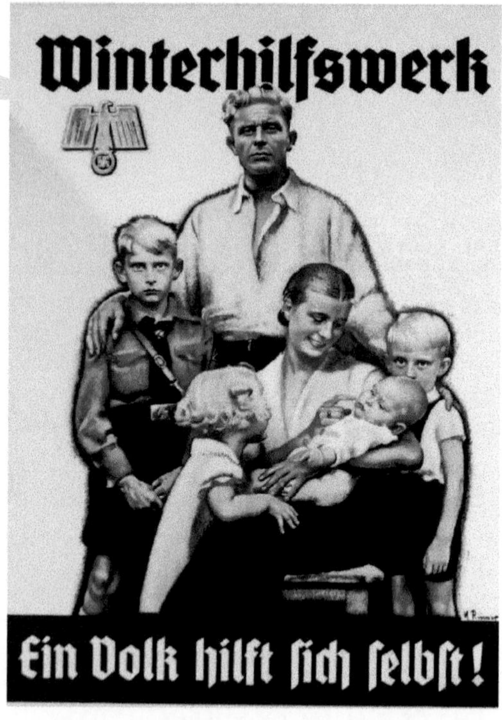

'Winter Relief Work: A People Helps Itself.' A Nazi poster from about 1938.

DAF also gave the German people rewards to make up for the things that they had lost with the end of the Weimar Republic. For example, although trade unions were now banned, the German Labour Front allowed workers to campaign for improved working conditions and they were given an extra day's holiday.

To get the benefits, all the workers had to do was give the Nazi state total **loyalty**. For people who had struggled through depression and unemployment, the DAF seemed like heaven – or did it?

It is hard to tell how many German workers just accepted being members of the DAF or if they actively supported Nazism. All the workers knew was that if they were not part of the DAF then it would be very difficult to find any job at all. As a result, most Germans kept their opinions to themselves and appeared to be good supporters of the Nazi state.

Within DAF there were three organisations that also kept most Germans on side with the Nazis.

GLOSSARY

Loyalty supporting something completely

Public works jobs created that are paid for by the government

Compulsory must be done

The Beauty of Work (SdA)

The SdA tried to make workplaces more attractive to workers. Old factories were freshened up and canteens where workers could get hot meals were opened. There were also smoke-free rooms and workplaces were kept much cleaner.

The Reich Labour Service (RAD)

The RAD made sure that everyone who wanted a job (and some who did not) had employment. When the Nazis came to power the number of unemployed was around six million. By 1939 the number of unemployed was tiny.

The Nazis greatly reduced youth unemployment, something European governments, including Britain's, try to do today. RAD provided a job for everyone aged between 16 and 25 years and that provided cheap workers for big **public works** schemes. In 1935 membership of RAD was **compulsory** for anyone who did not have a job elsewhere. Did young men complain about being forced to work on bridges and roads and schools? Some might not have liked it, but the work was welcomed by many. For the first time as adult workers, young men had a regular job and regular wages.

Strength Through Joy (KdF)

By far the most popular of the Nazi organisations was Strength Through Joy: *Kraft durch Freude* (KdF). KdF was popular simply because it provided people with leisure-time activities such as concerts, plays, libraries, day trips and holidays.

Nazi official statistics showed that in 1934, 2.3 million people took KdF holidays and by 1938 that number had increased to more than ten million. In fact, KdF became the world's largest tourism operator of the 1930s. Two cruise-liners were built to take members on trips to places such as Madeira and the coastline of Norway. In 1938 over 180,000 people went on these cruises.

German workers were also promised holidays and cars at a time when few people ever had such luxuries. Workers were encouraged to buy savings stamps and to put them into a collection book. When the book was full the workers would be able to exchange it for a Volkswagen Beetle car. In reality, no saver ever received a car due to war breaking out and military vehicles taking priority.

Encouraging savers to buy stamps towards a new car

A Strength Through Joy poster

How do these two posters make people want to join the Strength Through Joy organisation?

For most German workers, the 1930s under Hitler seemed to be better years than the 1920s under the Weimar Republic. At least that's what Nazi propaganda said. But how true was their claim of success?

How successful were Nazi economic policies?

Hitler's economic policy had two main targets:

1. **Full employment**. When the Nazis came to power the most serious problem was an unemployment rate of 26 per cent. The Nazis claimed that by 1939 there was full employment – everyone had a job.

> **GLOSSARY**
>
> **Full employment** everyone who wants a job has a job

2 Autarky. The Nazis wanted to make Germany **self-sufficient**. This meant that Germany would produce what it needed within Germany and would not rely on foreign imports.

GLOSSARY

Autarky the Nazi aim of self-sufficiency

Self-sufficient looking after yourself and not needing help from other countries

Germany's economic miracle the sudden improvement in Germany's economy in the 1930s

Were the targets met?

The answer to that question is both yes and no. It is true that Nazi Germany saw the biggest fall in unemployment of any country during the Great Depression. However, was that because of successful policies or because the unemployed were 'hidden'?

- The introduction of national service meant all young men spent six months in the German Labour Front and then they were conscripted into the army. By 1939, 1.4 million men were in the army, so they were not counted as unemployed.
- Many Jews were sacked and their jobs given to non-Jews. Jews were not counted as unemployed. The Nazis also took over a large amount of Jewish property and money. This boosted the economy but had nothing to do with Nazi economic policy.
- Many women were sacked and their jobs given to men. Women were not counted as unemployed.
- The Nazis stopped paying reparations which meant there was much more money to invest in the economy. This increased investment had nothing to do with Nazi economic policies.
- The Nazis took over other parts of Europe in the later 1930s such as Austria and parts of Czechoslovakia (present-day Czech Republic). The Nazis gained resources and raw materials from these countries but again this had nothing to do with Nazi economic policies.

Given the thousands of people who were not counted as unemployed by the Nazis and the resources the Nazis took from other countries, it is not surprising the Nazi policies appeared successful.

How does this poster show a Nazi version of its successful economic policies since coming to power?

Hitler's second aim – autarky – was a failure

While the Nazis tried to stop Germany from importing food, clothing and many other items, the amount of luxury items brought in for important Nazi officials kept increasing. For most Germans there were few luxury items available and everyday consumer goods were in short supply.

German scientists tried to make oil from coal and to find substitutes for rubber, petrol, cotton and coffee but were mostly unsuccessful.

Farmers were given subsidies (money) by the government to produce more food within Germany. Food imports were reduced, but food could have been imported much more cheaply from abroad.

So how true was the **German economic miracle**? For most Germans, the Nazis provided the one thing they really wanted – jobs. Hitler claimed to have cured unemployment. When Hitler became chancellor in 1933 unemployment stood at 26 per cent. By 1939 it stood at less than one per cent. The statistics were true, but few Germans really questioned how the fall in unemployment had been achieved. In fact it was hard and dangerous for most Germans to question anything in the Nazi state. It was easier just to go with the flow!

A representation of the Nazi regime's battle against unemployment

Activity 1

Summarise this chapter

The following summary reminds you of what this chapter has been about. Words that are important in this chapter have been made into ANAGRAMS. Your task is to sort out the anagrams then write the correct version of this summary into your workbook or work file.

Between 1933 and 1939 the German economy seemed to get much better. **NOUN EMPY MELT** *fell to almost nothing. The* **TURBAN FLOOR MANGER** *tried to organise all workers. It also provided leisure activities within the* **ENGTSH JOTH ROUGH TRY** *organisation. German workers could go on* **DAIYSLOH** *and hope to save money to buy a* **WAVGEN SOLK** *car. For most Germans, the main thing the Nazis did for them was to provide* **SOBJ** *and* **GESWA**.

Activity 2

The challenge! How far can you go?

The following questions go up in levels of difficulty in pairs. The first two are easy. The last two are hard. How many will you try to do?

1. Choose the two best answers to 'How did the German economy change once the Nazis took over?' from the following list:
   - Hyperinflation was still a problem.
   - Unemployment went up.
   - Unemployment went down.
   - More people were happy.
   - The Nazis failed to improve the economy.
2. Give reasons using some factual examples to support your choices in question 1.
3. Explain what Strength Through Joy was.
4. How would you summarise what is meant by a 'feel-good factor'?
5. What would you say was the importance of the German Labour Front?
6. Suppose you could make changes to the Nazi plans for the German economy. What would you do and why?

Activity 3

Work in pairs with each of you making up one 'describe' question and one 'explain' question based on the information in this chapter. Remember that these types of question are worth 4 or 6 marks. You must also make up a mark scheme to help someone mark the answer. Remember to include enough points in your mark scheme. Now exchange your questions with another pair and answer their questions.

After 10–12 minutes collect the answers to the questions you set. Mark the answers using your mark scheme. Give feedback to the person who answered your question. Feedback should be encouraging. Mention the good parts of the answer. Suggest ways the answer could be improved.

Question practice

National 4

Source A is from a recent school textbook.

SOURCE A

The Strength Through Joy organisation was popular, but probably because of what it offered rather than being a Nazi organisation. For members, two cruise-liners were built to take German workers on trips to places such as Madeira and the coastline of Norway. In 1938 over 180,000 people went on such cruises.

Describe why many Germans were happy with the way that the Nazis ran the German economy. You should use Source A and your own knowledge.

Success criteria

Provide at least two factual points of information, or one developed piece of information, on why many Germans were happy with the way that the Nazis ran the German economy.

National 5

To what extent did Germans benefit from Hitler's economic policies? (9 marks)

To be successful in this type of question you must show a judgement by stating that Germans PARTLY benefited from Nazi economic policies and then include accurate and relevant detail showing how people did benefit. You must then balance your answer by showing how some Germans did not benefit and that some of the economic policies were not as successful as claimed.

The following is an example of a weak answer, although it does include five pieces of detail. It is weak because it does not try to organise them into a balanced answer. The final sentence gives an answer to the question, but it is not balanced and contradicts some of the points made in the rest of the answer, so it only gets 2 marks out of 9. Your task is to turn this into a much better answer with organisation, balance and comments relevant to the question.

Unemployment fell as a result of Hitler's economic policies. Hitler's war economy created many jobs in the armed forces and building tanks, ships and aircraft. Hitler also invested in big public works projects like the building of the autobahns. A lot of money was spent on big prestige projects – like fancy new government buildings. German workers soon found that their wages were lower than before. Hitler introduced an efficient 'command economy' where there was careful planning and strikes were not allowed. Hitler's economic policies were of little benefit to the Germans.

Glossary

A

Abdicated – when the Kaiser gave up his power
Acquiescence – accepting something
Anti-Semitism – hostility against Jews
Article 48 – a law allowing the president to rule Germany in an emergency
Aryan – the German ideal of a north European, blonde-haired, blue-eyed master race
Autarky – the Nazi aim of self-sufficiency
Autobahn – the German motorway system

B

Boycott – refusing to use/buy something with the purpose of hurting the owner
Brownshirts – the Nazi Party's private army

C

Censored – information that is cut, restricted or withheld
Censorship – controlling news and information so that Germans knew only what the Nazis wanted them to know
Chancellor – the leader of the German government
Coalitions – political parties working together to form a government
Compulsory – must be done
Concentration camps – prisons for anyone who opposed the Nazis
Concordat – an agreement made between the Nazis and the Catholic Church in 1933
Constitution – a set of rules for running a country

D

Dachau – the first Nazi concentration camp
Dagger – a small knife designed for fighting
Dictatorship – a political system with one person or political party in total control and no opposition allowed
Diktat – linked to the English word 'dictated', it means Germans felt the treaty was forced on them, with no chance to discuss it

E

Ebert, Friedrich – leader of the Social Democratic Party and head of the Provisional Government
Enabling Act – gave Hitler the power to act as a dictator for four years

F

'Feel-good factor' – when the population of a country feel cheerful and politicians can take advantage of that to gain support
Freikorps – battle-hardened ex-soldiers who hated Communists or Spartacists
Full employment – everyone who wants a job has a job
Fundamental Laws – the basic laws of the Weimar Republic that guaranteed Germans their civil rights

G

Genocide – the deliberate wiping out (annihilation) of an entire race of people
German Christian Church – a new, Nazi-approved Christian church led by Ludwig Müller, the 'Reich Bishop'
German Confessional Church – a new Christian church against the Nazis led by Martin Niemöller

Germany's economic miracle – the sudden improvement in Germany's economy in the 1930s
Gestapo – the Nazis' secret state police force
Goebbels, Joseph – the man in charge of propaganda in Nazi Germany
Golden age – a time when things went very well; the Weimar Republic had a golden age between 1924 and 1929
Great Depression – a time of worldwide, high unemployment following an economic collapse in the USA starting in 1929

H

Hitler Jugend – Hitler Youth, a paramilitary group for German boys
Hyperinflation – sudden collapse in the value of German money

I

Indoctrination – making people believe and think what you want them to

J

Juden – German word for Jews

K

Kaiser – the emperor of Germany, Wilhelm II
Kristallnacht – an organised attack on Jews across Germany on the night of 9–10 November 1938
Krupp's – a German company making very strong steel

L

Landsberg – the prison where Hitler served his sentence after the *Putsch*
Left wing – people who wanted revolution and power to the working classes
Locarno Treaty – a 1925 treaty in which Germany tried to make better relations with its neighbours
Loyalty – supporting something completely

M

Mein Kampf – Hitler's autobiography, written while he was in prison
Monarchy – a political system with a royal family at its head
Mutiny – when soldiers and sailors refuse to follow orders
Myth – something that is believed to be true by lots of people but is really untrue

N

National Assembly – the name of the Parliament in the Weimar Republic
National Socialist German Workers' Party – the full name of the Nazi Party
Nationalists – people who wanted Germany to be stronger and have revenge for the Treaty of Versailles
Night of the Long Knives – on 30 June 1934, Hitler arranged for the murder of anyone he believed was a threat to him

O

Oath – a very serious promise

P

Pagan – not believing in the God of the Bible, Torah or Koran
Passive resistance – resisting by refusing to work for the French
Persecution – picking on people or extreme bullying; mistreatment
Plebiscite – a referendum or vote by the people about one question

Propaganda – influencing people with a simple, one-sided argument
Proportional representation – a voting system that assigns seats in proportion to the votes cast
Provisional Government – a temporary government created until full elections could take place
Public works – jobs created that are paid for by the government
Putsch – German word for an armed takeover of power

R

Reichsbank – the main German bank
Rentenmarks – new German currency to replace the worthless old money
Reparations – compensation that Germany had to pay for causing the war
Republic – a political system with no royal family
Resistance – being against something
Revolution – a big change in a political system, when the old system is completely overthrown, usually by violence
Right wing – people who did not want change and, in fact, wanted power to go back to the Kaiser and the upper classes
Ruhr – a heavily industrialised region of western Germany
Rust, Bernhard – head of German education

S

SA – *Sturmabteilung*, the Nazi private army, also known as the Brownshirts
Scapegoat – something/someone to blame things on
Self-sufficient – looking after yourself and not needing help from other countries
Soviet – a local council made up of soldiers, sailors and workers to rule their own areas
Spartacists – revolutionaries who wanted to make Germany into a Communist state
SS – Hitler's personal bodyguards that grew to the size of an army
Stabbed in the back – betrayed; some Germans felt they had lost the war because they had been stabbed in the back by revolutionaries back home
Swastika – the Nazi badge or logo
Synagogues – Jewish places of worship

T

Totalitarian state – a state that controls everything and does not allow opposition

V

Versailles – a palace near Paris where the peace treaty ending the First World War was signed
Vice-chancellor – the second in command to the chancellor
von Ludendorff, Erich – a military hero of the First World War who reminded many people of the 'good old days' of the Kaiser

W

Wall Street Crash – the Great Depression started with the collapse of the US stock market based in Wall Street, New York
War guilt – part of the Treaty of Versailles which claimed that Germany had caused the war and so was also to blame for all the death and destruction it produced
Weimar – a town in central Germany
Weimar constitution – the rules set up to run the new Weimar Republic

Index